Adventures in the Torah

Student Book

Kingdom Kids Messianic Children's Program

Written by Judy Rich | Illustrated by Austin Worland

Adventures in the Torah: Messianic Children's Program, Student Book

Messianic Kids
messianickids.com

ISBN: 979-8-89217-066-6

First Edition

Designed by Judy Rich

Hello & Welcome!

Welcome to Adventures in the Torah with Kingdom Kids! We're so glad you're here, learning God's word with us.

With your class, you're going to be learning about the Torah this year, studying through each of the Torah portions (which were divided by Torah scholars over two thousand years ago to read every Shabbat). Each week you'll learn about what the Torah teaches and how you can apply it in your own life.

Each week you'll be given a memory verse that you can work on memorizing at home with your parents. You'll also learn more about what it looks life to have godly character and get to practice that in your life with your family and friends.

We're excited to see what our Father has in store for you this year!

. . . .

Parents! We are so excited that your child is taking on the study of the Torah this year. While the Torah can feel overwhelming at times, we believe that since it sets the foundation for all of Scripture, it's very important to understand! We're committed to making the study of Torah engaging and fun for your kids, and our prayer is that it will breath life into your home.

Each week your child will be using this book to reinforce what they are learning at their Shabbat School, memorizing verses from throughout the Bible and learning to apply godly character in their lives. We encourage you to stay engaged with what they are learning to make the most of their lessons at home. Praying you have a wonderful year!

Judy Kiol

Before We Get Started...

In our classes this year, we are going to be learning about the Torah, the first five books of the Bible. The Bible was written by God, through people who had a relationship with Him and in whom God's Spirit dwelled.

What does that mean?

To dwell means to live. Did you know that when we give our lives to God, He saves us and lives within us?

Isn't that amazing? The Creator of the whole universe lives within us when we give our lives to Him.

What does it mean for us to give our lives to Him? What does it mean to be saved?

The Bible tells us that all people have sinned (Romans 3:23) and that sin causes punishment and ultimately death (Romans 6:23). However, through Messiah Yeshua, God made a way for us to be made right forever before Him (John 3:16-17). Yeshua's death paid the price forever for our sin.

But in order for His sacrifice to count for each of us, we all have to make a choice to accept what He did for us. When we do, we will receive eternal life through a relationship with God forever (Colossians 2:13-15).

How do we do that? The Bible says it's pretty simple:

> "For if you confess with your mouth that Yeshua is Lord, and believe in your heart that God raised Him from the dead, you will be saved." *- Romans 10:9*

We are to say that Yeshua is Lord, which means master *(someone who is in charge over you)*, and believe that He rose from the dead. When we believe that He is who He says He is, and give Him control of our lives, that choice begins our relationship with God!

Once we have a relationship with God, God will help us live better for Him by His Spirit that lives within us. The Torah tells us the two most important commandment - rules - that God has for us:

1. Love God with all your heart, soul, mind, and strength.

2. Love your neighbor *(that's all the people around you)* like you love yourself.

The rest of the Bible gives us all kinds of ideas of what it looks like to do those two things in our lives. And that is what we're going to be learning all about this year.

But it all starts with having a relationship with God.

If you've already made that choice - yay! We hope this book helps you grow closer to God.

If you haven't made it yet, that's okay! We hope this book helps you see how wonderful God is and that at some point you will decide to give your life to God. Feel free to talk to your parents or your teacher, and they will help answer any questions you have as you make the most important decision of your life!

Welcome to the adventure!

Unit 1: B'resheet | Genesis

Welcome to your first unit of Adventures in the Torah with Kingdom Kids! We're glad you're here.

If you haven't read the introduction, you can do that now (or even better - have your parent read it with you!) so that you know what to expect in this book.

The first book of the Torah is Genesis, or in Hebrew, *B'resheet*. That's pronounced *beh-rey-**sheet***. *B'resheet* means "In the beginning". In this book, you'll find the stories about the created world's beginnings and the establishment of God's people in the families of Abraham, Isaac, and Jacob.

The stories in Genesis take place over the span of about 2500 years - a very large chunk of time in which most people lived a lot longer than we do now! Do you know how long the oldest person lived? That was Methuselah, and he lived 969 years!

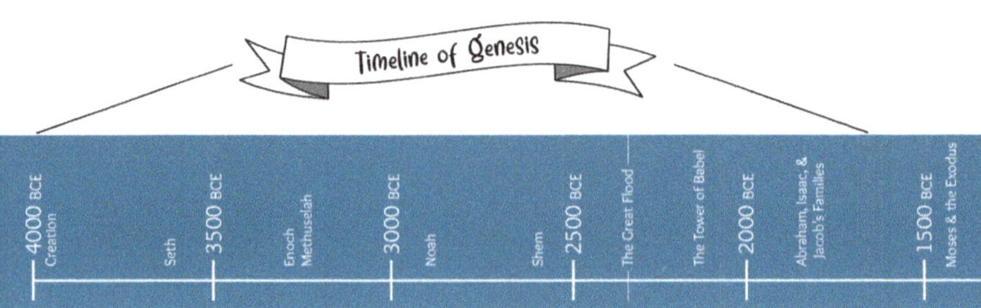

During this unit you will also learn the most central of all prayers in Judaism - the *Shema*. *Shema* means "listen & do" and this prayer is taken from Deuteronomy 6:4-9.

You'll also learn some commonly-used Hebrew words and memorize lots of verses from Scripture. Let's go!

Main Characters of Genesis:

God {HaShem} - Our Father in Heaven is the main character of all of Scripture, but especially Genesis! The beginning of history is the beginning of His story for humanity.

Adam - the first man, created by God, and his wife, Eve

Noah - the man who built the ark to save his family during the great flood

Abraham - the man whom God chose to begin the family of His chosen people, eventually to be called the Hebrews, Israelites and then the Jews

Isaac - Abraham's son, who was promised to him long before he was born

Jacob - Isaac's younger son, through whom God established His people

Joseph - Jacob's favorite son, the oldest of his second wife, Rachel, through whom God saved the entire clan of Jacob's descendents

–Beresheet–

Genesis 1:1-6:8 | Creation & the Fall

God Created the World

This week we learned about the creation of the world, and especially the first two people. We learned that Adam & Eve sinned by disobeying God. As a consequence of sin entering the world, life became much harder for humanity.

But God also has a solution which enables us to live forever with Him in eternity!

I've learned my Memory Verse!

Simple

"In the beginning God created the heavens and the earth." *Gensis 1:1*

Complete

"In the beginning God created the heavens and the earth." Genesis 1:1 "So the heavens and the earth were completed along with their entire array. God completed - on the seventh day - His work that He made, and He ceased - on the seventh day - from all His work that He made." Genesis 2:1-2

Teacher/Parent's Signature

I'm Practicing Godly Character!

This week we learned about **Love**. Love is treating others the way we want to be treated. All other character traits build on love!

Here's how I practiced love this week:

____

____

____

We learned to say our first Hebrew word:

Hello/peace: *shalom* (shah-LOAM)

שלום

During this unit, we are going to learn the most central and important prayer in Judaism - the *Shema*. *Shema* means "listen and do". Here are the first few words:

"Shema Yisrael Adonai Eloheinu, Adonai echad."
"Hear, Israel - The Lord our God, the Lord is one."

Hebrew Names & Dates from This Week:

HaShem = God (This means "The Name" and is a way to refer to God without using His most holy name)
Chava = Eve

- - - - - - - - - -

The date & location of the Eden story are unkonwn but likely around 4000BCE.

Hebrew & Liturgy Review

–Noach–

Genesis 6:9-11:32 | The Great Flood

Our Choices Have Consequences

This week we learned about Noah, the man of God who built an ark to survive the flood that God sent to punish mankind.

We learned that there are good and bad consequences for our actions and that obeying God is always a smart thing to do!

I've Learned My Memory Verse!

SIMPLE

"The fear of ADONAI is the beginning of knowledge, but fools despise wisdom and discipline." *Proverbs 1:7*

COMPLETE

"The fear of ADONAI is the beginning of knowledge, but fools despise wisdom and discipline. Hear, my son, your father's instruction and forsake not your mother's teaching. For they are a garland of grace for your head and a chain to adorn your neck." *Proverbs 1:7-9*

____

Teacher/Parent's Signature

I'm Practicing Godly Character!

This week we learned about **Gratitude**.
Gratitude means being thankful for
everything that we have.

Here's how I practiced gratitude this week:

____

____

____

We learned to say our second Hebrew word:

Good morning: *Boker Tov (BO-kehr TOV)*

בּוֹקֶר טוֹב

And we learned the second line of the *Shema*:

"Baruch shem k'vod malchuto l'olam va'ed."

"Blessed be His name, whose glorious kingdom
is forever and ever."

Hebrew Names & Dates from This Week:

Noach = Noah

- - - - - - - - - -

*Dating for the flood is unclear, but most believe it
happened −2400BCE.*

~Lech Lecha~

Genesis 12:1-17:27 | Avram's Call

We Can Trust God

This week we were introduced to Avram & Sarai, the father and mother of our faith. We learned about how Avram obeyed God to travel to wherever God sent him.

God promised to bless Avram with a son, and through his descendants He would make a nation. But Avram & Sarai had to wait a long time and trust God for that promised child!

I've Learned My Memory Verse!

SIMPLE

"In you all the families of the earth will be blessed." *Genesis 12:3b*

COMPLETE

"My heart's desire is to make you into a great nation, to bless you, to make your name great so that you may be a blessing. My desire is to bless those who bless you, but whoever curses you I will curse, and in you all the families of the earth will be blessed." *Genesis 12:2-3*

____

Teacher/Parent's Signature

I'm Practicing Godly Character!

This week we learned about **Patience**.
Patience means waiting with a good attitude.

Here's how I practiced patience this week:

____

____

____

We learned to say a new Hebrew word:

Thank you: *todah* (toh-DAH)

תּוֹדָה

We started learned the verses in Deuteronomy 6:5-9 that are said right after the *Shema*. We start here:

"You shall love the Lord your God with all your heart, with all your soul, and with all your might."

Hebrew Names & Dates from This Week:

Avram = Abram   *Avraham = Abraham*

- - - - - - - - - -

Today's story took place in Canaan in ~1950BCE.

–Vayera–

Genesis 18:1-22:24 | Avraham's Testing

God Keeps His Promises

This week we continued learning about Avraham & Sarah. God gave them the son He had promised them - Isaac. One day when Isaac was grown, God tested Avraham's faith by asking Him to sacrifice Isaac. God made a way to save Isaac's life, but used that time to grow Avraham's faith! We also learned how God punished sin by destroying Sodom & Gomorrah.

I've Learned My Memory Verse!

SIMPLE

"Trust in ADONAI with all your heart, lean not on your own understanding."
Proverbs 3:5

COMPLETE

"Trust in ADONAI with all your heart, lean not on your own understanding. In all your ways acknowledge Him, and He will make your paths straight. Do not be wise in your own eyes; fear ADONAI and turn away from evil." *Proverbs 3:5-7*

____

Teacher/Parent's Signature

I'm Practicing Godly Character!

This week we learned about **Honesty**.
Honesty is being totally truthful about things.

Here's how I practiced honesty this week:

____

____

____

We learned to say two new Hebrew words:

You're welcome & Please:
bevakasha (beh-vah-kah-SHAH)

בְּבַקָשָׁה

We kept learned the verses in Deuteronomy 6:5-9 that are said right after the *Shema*:

"And these words which I command you today shall be on your heart."

HEBREW NAMES & DATES FROM THIS WEEK:

Avraham=Abraham   Yitzhak = Isaac

- - - - - - - - - -

Today's story took place in Canaan in ~1850BCE.

–Chayei Sarah–

Genesis 23:1-25:18 | Rebekah is Chosen

God Helps Us Make Good Choices

This week we learned about how Avraham sent his most trusted servant to find a wife for Isaac after Sarah died. The servant, Eliezer, asked for God's guidance to find the right woman, and when he found Rebekah, she was willing to come back to Canaan with him to marry Isaac.

I've learned my Memory Verse!

SIMPLE

"You guide me with Your counsel." *Psalm 73:24a*

COMPLETE

"You guide me with Your counsel, and afterward You will take me into glory. Whom have I in heaven but You? On earth there is none I desire besides You. My flesh and my heart may fail, but God is the strength of my heart and my portion forever." *Psalm 73:24-26*

____

Teacher/Parent's Signature

I'm Practicing Godly Character!

This week we learned about **Responsibility**. Responsibility means being trustworthy and reliable.

Here's how I practiced responsibility this week:

____

____

____

We reviewed our last 4 Hebrew words:

shalom   שָׁלוֹם   hello/peace

boker tov   בֹּקֶר טוֹב   good morning

todah   תּוֹדָה   thank you

bevakasha   בְּבַקָשָׁה   please/you're welcome

And we continued learning the verses in Deuteronomy that are recited after the *Shema*:

"You shall teach them dilligently to your children."

HEBREW NAMES & DATES FROM THIS WEEK:

Avraham=Abraham   Yitzhak = Isaac

Rivkah = Rebekah

- - - - - - - - - -

Today's story took place in Canaan in ~1811 BCE.

–Toldot–

Genesis 25:19-28:9 | Jacob & Esau

God Has Plans for Us

This week we learned about Isaac & Rebekah's twin sons - Jacob & Esau. We learned that Esau sold his birthright to Jacob for a pot of stew and Jacob tricked his father into giving him Esau's blessing.

In the end, we learned that God wants to use each of us for His plans!

I've learned my Memory Verse!

SIMPLE

"Before I formed you in the womb, I knew you, and before you were born, I set you apart." *Jeremiah 1:5a*

COMPLETE

"Before I formed you in the womb, I knew you, and before you were born, I set you apart — I appointed you prophet to the nations... Do not say 'I'm only a boy!' For to everyone I send you, you will go, and all I command you, you will speak." *Jeremiah 1:5 & 7*

____

Teacher/Parent's Signature

I'm Practicing Godly Character!

This week we learned about **Integrity**.
Integrity means doing what is right, even when no one sees.

Here's how I practiced integrity this week:

____

____

____

We learned to say two new Hebrew words:

Yes: *ken (kehn)*   No: *lo (low)*

כֵּן   לֹא

And we learned more of the verses that are recited right after the *Shema*:

"You shall talk of them when you sit in your house and when you walk on the way - when you lie down and when you rise up."

Hebrew Names & Dates from This Week:

Yitzhak = Isaac   Rivkah = Rebekah
Ya'akov = Jacob   Esav = Esau

- - - - - - - - - -

Today's story took place in Canaan in ~1760 BCE.

–Vayishlach–

Genesis 28:10-32:2 | Jacob Forms a Family

God Provides Our Needs

This week we learned about what happened when Jacob left home. He ended up at his uncle Laban's house, married two of his daughters (that's quite a story!) and had 11 children born!

God blessed Jacob abundantly and he grew quite wealthy by raising flocks of sheep for Laban as his family grew.

I've learned my Memory Verse!

Simple

"Adonai is my shepherd, I shall not want."
Psalm 23:1

Complete

"Adonai is my shepherd, I shall not want. He makes me lie down in green pastures. He leads me beside still waters. He restores my soul. He guides me in paths of righteousness for His Name's sake."
Psalm 23:1-3

____

Teacher/Parent's Signature

I'm Practicing Godly Character!

This week we learned about **Joyfulness**. Joyfulness is a good feeling in your heart that comes from God and not your circumstances.

Here's how I practiced joyfulness this week:

____

____

____

We learned to say a new Hebrew word:

Good job: *kol hakavod (kohl ha-ka-VODE)*

כֹּל הַכָּבוֹד

And we learned more of the verses that are recited right after the *Shema*:

"You shall bind them as a sign on your hand, and they shall be as frontlets between your eyes."

Hebrew Names & Dates from This Week:

Lavan = Laban   Ya'akov = Jacob
Rachel = (pronounced rah-chell)

- - - - - - - - - -

Today's story took place in Canaan in ~1700 BCE.

–Vayishlach–

Genesis 32:3-36:43 | Jacob Wrestles with God

God Helps Us Be Brave

This week we learned that time had come for Jacob's family to leave Lavan's home and go back to Canaan. Ya'akov was still afraid of his brother, Esau's anger. One night, God came to Ya'akov and wrestled with him all night. Through this, God blessed him and gave him the courage to face Esau, who wasn't angry with him anymore!

I've learned my Memory Verse!

SIMPLE

"For God has not given us a spirit of fear but of power and love and self-discipline."
2 Timothy 1:7

COMPLETE

"For God has not given us a spirit of fear but of power and love and self-discipline."
2 Timothy 1:7

"Have I not commanded you? *Chazak!* Be strong! Do not be terrified or dismayed, for Adonai your God is with you wherever you go." *Joshua 1:9*

____

Teacher/Parent's Signature

I'm Practicing Godly Character!

This week we learned about **Courage**.
Courage is the choice to do really hard, painful, or even scary things.

Here's how I practiced courage this week:

____

____

____

Hebrew & Liturgy Review

We learned to say a new Hebrew word:
Good-bye: *lehitra'ot (leh-HEET-rah-OHT)*

לְהִתְרָאוֹת

And we finished learning the verses that are recited right after the *Shema*:

"You shall write them on the doorposts of your house and on your gates."

Hebrew Names & Dates from This Week:

Ya'akov = Jacob   *Esav = Esau*

Today's story took place in Canaan in ~1700BCE.

–Vayeshev–

Genesis 37:1-40:23 | Joseph's Boyhood

God is *El Roi* - God Who Sees

This week we shifted from Jacob to Joseph! Yosef was Jacob's favorite son, his firstborn from Rachel. One day, Jacob's older sons secretly sold Joseph into slavery in Egypt. As a slave, Yosef worked hard and didn't forget God - he kept doing what was right and God saw his struggle and his obedience!

I've learned my Memory Verse!

SIMPLE

"You searched me and know me."
Psalm 139:1

COMPLETE

"You searched me and know me. Whenever I sit down or stand up, You know it. You discern my thinking from afar. You observe my journeying and my resting and You are familiar with all my ways." *Psalm 139:1-3*

____

Teacher/Parent's Signature

I'm Practicing Godly Character!

This week we learned about **Respect**. Respectfulness is caring how your words and actions may affect others.

Here's how I practiced respect this week:

____

____

____

We learned to say a new Hebrew word:

Quietly/Be quiet: *besheket (beh-SHEH-keht)*

בְּשֶׁקֶט

And we reviewed the *Shema*:

"Shema Yisrael Adonai Eloheinu, Adonai echad. Baruch shem k'vod malchuto l'olam va'ed."

"Hear, Israel - The Lord our God, the Lord is one. Blessed be His name, whose glorious kingdom is forever and ever."

Hebrew Names & Dates from This Week:

Yosef=Joseph

- - - - - - - - - -

Today's story took place in Canaan & Egypt around 1683 BCE.

–Miketz–

Genesis 41:1-44:17 | Joseph Leads Egypt

We Can Be Lights for God

This week we learned about Joseph's rise to power in Egypt! Because he interpreted Pharaoh's dreams, he was given lots of power to help save Egypt from a coming famine.

Years later, Yosef's brothers came to buy food, but didn't regognize him. We'll find out what happens next week!

I've learned my Memory Verse!

Simple

"You are the light of the world."
Matthew 5:14a

Complete

"You are the light of the world. A city set on a hill cannot be hidden. Neither do people light a lamp and put it under a basket. Instead, they put it on a lampstand so it gives light to all in the house. In the same way, let your light shine before men so they may see your good works and glorify your Father in heaven." *Matthew 5:14-16*

____
Teacher/Parent's Signature

I'm Practicing Godly Character!

This week we learned about **Contentment**. Contentment is being happy regardless of your situation.

Here's how I practiced contentment this week:

____

____

____

Hebrew & Liturgy Review

Hebrew Names & Dates from This Week:

Yosef=Joseph

- - - - - - - - - -

Today's story took place in Egypt around 1663 BCE.

—Vayigash—

Genesis 44:18-47:27 | Joseph Forgives His Brothers

God Wants Us to Forgive

This week we learned about how Joseph forgave his brothers for the terrible way they treated him years before. Before this happened, though, he tested them to see if they truly regretted what they did.

After he told them who he was, Yosef invited their entire clan to live in the best land of Egypt for the rest of the famine!

I've Learned My Memory Verse!

SIMPLE

"Be kind to one another, compassionate, forgiving each other."
Ephesians 4:32

COMPLETE

"Be kind to one another, compassionate, forgiving each other just as God in Messiah also forgave you."
Ephesians 4:32

____

Teacher/Parent's Signature

I'm Practicing Godly Character!

This week we learned about **Forgiveness**. Forgiveness starts when we let go of the hurt someone caused us and don't hold a grudge.

Here's how I practiced forgiveness this week:

____

____

____

We learned to say a new Hebrew phrase:

It's time for a snack:
zman lechatif (zmahn leh-chah-TEEF)

זְמַן לְחָטִיף

And we continued reviewing the *Shema*:

"You shall teach them dilligently to your children. You shall talk of them when you sit in your house and when you walk on the way, when you lie down and when you rise up."

Hebrew Names & Dates from This Week:

Ya'akov = Jacob   *Yosef = Joseph*

Today's story took place in Egypt in ~1661 BCE.

–Vayechi–

Genesis 47:28-50:26 | The End of Jacob's Life

You Have a Role in God's Kingdom

This week we learned about how Ya'akov blessed all of his sons before he died. He saw that each of his sons would some day become a tribe and gave them each a role to play in the big picture. Jacob remembered God's promise to his grandfather Avraham and knew God had something big in store for his family!

I've learned My Memory Verse!

Simple

"You are the body of Messiah, and members individually." *1 Corinthians 12:27*

Complete

"You are the body of Messiah, and members individually." *1 Corinthians 12:27*

"God has placed the parts—each one of them—in the body just as He desired. If they were all one part, where would the body be? But now there are many parts, yet one body." *1 Corinthians 12:18-20*

____

Teacher/Parent's Signature

I'm Practicing Godly Character!

This week we learned about **Peacefulness**.
Peace means calm and wholeness inside of
you regardless of the circumstances.

Here's how I practiced peacefulness this week:

____

____

____

Hebrew & Liturgy Review

We learned to say a new Hebrew phrase:

It's time to clean up:
zman lenakot (zmahn leh-nah-KOTE)

זְמַן לְנַקּוֹת

And we finished reviewing the *Shema*:

"You shall bind them as a sign on your hand,
and they shall be as frontlets between your eyes.
You shall write them on the doorposts of your
house and on your gates."

Hebrew Names & Dates from This Week:

Ya'akov = Jacob   *Shaul = Paul*
- - - - - - - - - -
Today's story took place in Egypt in ~1644 BCE.

Unit 2: Shemot | Exodus

Welcome to your second unit of Adventures in the Torah! We hope you had fun learning about the beginnings of the world in Genesis. God began a lot of things in Genesis - not only the world itself, but He began forming His chosen people through Abraham.

The second book of the Torah is Exodus, or in Hebrew, *Shemot*. That's pronounced *sheh-**moat**. Shemot* means "Names". In this book, you'll find the stories about how God frees His chosen people from slavery to Egypt to instead serve and worship Him.

The stories in Genesis took place over the span of about 2500 years, but the stories in Exodus all take place over about 80 years. There is a long gap between the books, however, when the descendants of Jacob grow in number in Egypt and eventually become enslaved by a pharaoh who didn't remember the way Joseph saved them from famine long ago.

A Closer look at the Exodus & Wandering:

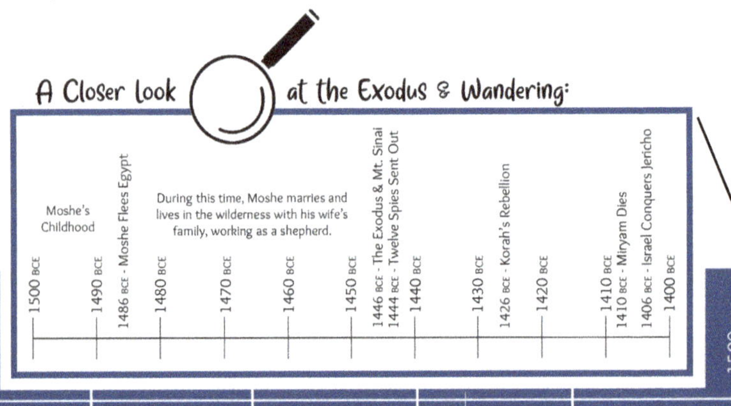

During this unit you will also learn the most central prayer in the Apostolic Scriptures that our Messiah Yeshua taught - the *Avinu* (Our Father).

You'll also learn some commonly-used Hebrew words and memorize lots of verses from Scripture. Let's go!

Main Characters of Exodus:

God {HaShem} - Our Father in Heaven is the main character of all of Scripture, but in Exodus we see how He freed His people from slavery in order to serve Him alone

Moses - born into slavery but raised as Egyptian royalty, Moses (Moshe) was the man God used to free the Hebrews from slavery

Aaron - Moses' older brother, who God called to help Moses speak clearly and bravely to Pharaoh

Miriam - Moses and Aaron's sister, who saved Moses' life as a baby and helped lead the Hebrews as a prophetess when she grew up

Pharaoh - the antagonist of the Exodus story, a leader in Egypt who didn't want to let God's people leave but wanted to keep them enslaved

Joshua - Moses' assistant after they left Egypt

–Shemot–

Exodus 1:1-6:1 | The Calling of Moses

God Is Compassionate

This week we began the book of Exodus! Beginning with the story of baby Moses being saved in a basket in the Nile River, we saw how God guided his life in special ways until He revealed to Moses what His purpose was for his life.

At a burning bush in the desert, God called Moses to set His people free from slavery!

I've learned My Memory Verse!

Simple

"ADONAI is gracious and compassionate, slow to anger and great in loving-kindness." *Psalm 145:8*

Complete

"ADONAI is gracious and compassionate, slow to anger and great in loving-kindness. ADONAI is good to all. He has compassion on all His creatures." *Psalm 145:8-9*

____

Teacher/Parent's Signature

I'm Practicing Godly Character!

This week we learned about **Compassion**.
Compassion is feeling sad for other people's struggles and wanting to help.

Here's how I practiced compassion this week:

____

____

____

We learned to say a new Hebrew phrase:

It's time for Hebrew:
zman le'ivreet (zmahn leh-ee-VREET)

זְמַן לְעִבְרִית

And we began learning the prayer Yeshua taught His disciples, the *Avinu* (Our Father):

"Avinu shebashamayim yitkadesh shmecha."
"Our Father who is in heaven, may your name be sanctified."

Hebrew Names & Dates from This Week:

Moshe = Moses   Miryam = Miriam
- - - - - - - - - -
Today's story took place in both Egypt and Midian between ~1526-1446 BCE.

-Va'era-

Exodus 6:2-9:35 | The Plagues

We Need to Yield to God

This week we talked about what happened after God called Moses to go back to Egypt with his brother, Aaron. Pharaoh didn't let the Hebrews go, so God sent 10 terrible plagues on Egypt as a punishment and a show of His great power.

As the plagues got worse, the only affected the Egyptians, showing God's mercy on His people.

I've learned my Memory Verse!

Simple

"Children, obey your parents in the Lord, for this is right." *Ephesians 6:1*

Complete

"Children, obey your parents in the Lord, for this is right. Honor your father and mother (which is the first commandment with a promise), so that it may be well with you, and you may live long on the earth." *Ephesians 6:1-3*

____

Teacher/Parent's Signature

I'm Practicing Godly Character!

This week we learned about **Submission**.
Submission is when we yield to an authority over us, like parents or teachers.

Here's how I practiced submission this week:

____

____

____

We learned to say a new Hebrew phrase:
It's time for Torah:
zman letorah (zmahn leh-toe-RAH)

זְמַן לְתוֹרָה

And we continued learning the *Avinu*:

"Tavo malchutecha, y'aseh retzonecha ka'asher bashamayim gam b'aretz."
"May your kingdom come; as your will is done in heaven, may it also be on earth."

Hebrew Names & Dates from This Week:

Moshe = Moses   Aharon = Aaron

- - - - - - - - - -

Today's story took place in Egypt in ~1446 BCE.

-Bo-

Exodus 10:1-13:16 | The Passover

Yeshua is Our Passover Lamb

This week we learned about the last plague on Egypt and the Passover - the meal that the Hebrews ate while God passed over their homes with the last plague. After that, Pharaoh let the Hebrews leave Egypt at last! We also talked about how Yeshua is our Passover lamb and provided our freedom from slavery to sin!

I've learned My Memory Verse!

SIMPLE

"For everyone who calls upon the name of Adonai shall be saved." *Romans 10:13*

COMPLETE

"If you confess with your mouth that Yeshua is Lord, and believe in your heart that God raised Him from the dead, you will be saved. For with the heart it is believed for righteousness, and with the mouth it is confessed for salvation...For everyone who calls upon the name of Adonai shall be saved." *Romans 10:9-10,13*

____

Teacher/Parent's Signature

I'm Practicing Godly Character!

This week we learned about **Faithfulness**.
Faithfulness means being trustworthy and loyal, especially to God.

Here's how I practiced faithfulness this week:

____

____

____

We reviewed our last four Hebrew phrases:

zman lechatif	זְמַן לְחַטִיף	time for snack
zman lenakot	זְמַן לְנַקּוֹת	time to clean up
zman ley'ivreet	זְמַן לְעִבְרִית	time for Hebrew
zman letorah	זְמַן לְתוֹרָה	time for Torah

And we continued learning the *Avinu:*

"*Et lechem chukenu ten lanu hayom*"
"Give us the bread that is our allotment today…"

Hebrew Names & Dates from This Week:

Moshe = Moses   *Aharon = Aaron*

- - - - - - - - - -

Today's story took place in Egypt in ~1446 BCE.

LESSON 16

–Beshalach–

Exodus 13:17-17:16 | Crossing the Red Sea

God is Our Protector

A few days after Moses led the people out of Egypt, Pharaoh regretted letting them go and started coming after them. He caught up with them as they were stuck at the Red Sea. However, God worked a miracle for the Hebrews and split the Red Sea! The Israelites walked across dry land and the Egyptians drowned trying to chase them - God's people were free at last!

I've learned my Memory Verse!

Simple

"Since Adonai is at my right hand, I will not be shaken." *Psalm 16:8b*

Complete

"I have set Adonai always before me. Since He is at my right hand, I will not be shaken. So my heart is glad and my soul rejoices. My body also rests secure." *Psalm 16:8-9*

____

Teacher/Parent's Signature

I'm Practicing Godly Character!

This week we learned about **Meekness**.
Meekness means holding back when you are strong, standing confident.

Here's how I practiced meekness this week:

____

____

____

We learned to say a new Hebrew phrase:
How are you? (to a boy & girl):

boy: *ma shlomcha (mah shlom-CHAH)* מַה שְׁלוֹמְךָ

girl: *ma shlomech (mah shlo-MECH)* מַה שְׁלוֹמֵךְ

And we continued learning the Avinu:

*"U'mechal lanu al chovoteinu, ka-asher machalnu
gam anachnu lechayaveinu."*
"Pardon us our debts as we also have pardoned
those indebted to us."

Hebrew Names & Dates from This Week:

Moshe = Moses   Miryam = Miriam

- - - - - - - - - -

Today's story took place outside Egypt in
~1446 BCE.

–Yitro–

Exodus 18:1-20:23 | The 10 Commandments

God's Rules are Good for Us

This week we learned that after a couple months of travel, being led by a cloud during the day and a fire by night, the Israelites came to Mount Sinai. God had been providing them manna to eat each day, and now He gave them the beginning of His perfect plan for them - the Ten Commandments!

I've Learned My Memory Verse!

SIMPLE

"You will be My own treasure from among all people." *Exodus 19:5*

COMPLETE

"'You have seen what I did to the Egyptians, and how I carried you on eagle's wings and brought you to Myself. Now then, if you listen closely to My voice, and keep My covenant, then you will be My own treasure from among all people, for all the earth is Mine.'"
Exodus 19:4-5

____
Teacher/Parent's Signature

I'm Practicing Godly Character!

This week we learned about **Orderliness**. Orderliness means doing the right things, the right way, at the right time.

Here's how I practiced orderliness this week:

____

____

____

We learned to say a new Hebrew phrase:

Good/Very Good!
tov/tov me'od (TOV / TOV meh-OD)

טוֹב מְאוֹד

And we continued learning the Avinu:

"V'al t'viyeinu lidei nisayon ki im tachaltzeinu min hara."
"Do not bring us into the hands of testing, but rescue us from what is evil."

Hebrew Names & Dates from This Week:

Moshe = Moses

- - - - - - - - - -

Today's story took place at the base of Mount Sinai in ~1446 BCE.

–Mishpatim–

Exodus 21:1-24:18 | God Gives the Torah

God Empowers Us to Obey His Rules

This week we learned that hearing God's voice scared the Israelites so much that they asked Moshe to go up on Mount Sinai and talk to God himself rather than have God speak to all of them! God promised that He would bless Israel if they obeyed the commands He gave Moses, and that He would be with them always.

I've learned my Memory Verse!

SIMPLE

"I will put My Torah within them, I will write it on their heart." *Jeremiah 31:32b*

COMPLETE

"I will put My Torah within them. Yes, I will write it on their heart. I will be their God and they will be My people. No longer will each teach his neighbor or each his brother, saying: 'Know Adonai,' for they will all know Me, from the least of them to the greatest.' It is a declaration of Adonai." *Jeremiah 31:32b-33a*

____

Teacher/Parent's Signature

I'm Practicing Godly Character!

This week we learned about **Kindness**.
Kindness is love in action, things we do in order to benefit others.

Here's how I practiced kindness this week:

____

____

____

We learned to say a new Hebrew phrase:
I'm happy! (from a boy & girl):

boy: *ani sameach* (ah-NEE sah-MEH-ach) אֲנִי שָׂמֵחַ

girl: *ani smecha* (ah-NEE smeh-CHAH) אֲנִי שְׂמֵחָה

And we continued learning the Avinu:

"Ki lecha hamamlecha v'hagevurah v'hatif'eret l'olmei olamim."
"For yours is the kingdom and the power and the majesty, forever and ever."

Hebrew Names & Dates from This Week:

Moshe = Moses

- - - - - - - - - -

Today's story took place at the base of Mount Sinai in ~1446 BCE.

–Terumah–

Exodus 25:1-27:19 | Instructions for the Tabernacle

We Want to Give God Our Best

This week we learned about the design God gave Moses for the Tabernacle - the special tent and area where God's people would gather to sacrifice and worship Him.

God wanted the best for His house of worship, and we want to give God the best of our lives too!

I've Learned My Memory Verse!

Simple

"Don't you know that you are God's temple?" *1 Corinthians 3:16a*

Complete

"Have them make a Sanctuary for Me, so that I may dwell among them."
Exodus 25:8

"Don't you know that you are God's temple and that the *Ruach Elohim* dwells among you?" *1 Corinthians 3:16*

____

Teacher/Parent's Signature

I'm Practicing Godly Character!

This week we learned about **Reverence.**
Reverence is a feeling of respect mixed with love that we apply mostly to "God things."

Here's how I practiced reverence this week:

____

____

____

We learned to say a new Hebrew phrase:
I'm sad! (from a boy & girl):
boy: *ani atzuv (ah-NEE ah-TZOOV)* אֲנִי עָצוּב
girl: *ani atzuva (ah-NEE ah-tzoo-VAH)* אֲנִי עֲצוּבָה

And we reviewed the first part of the *Avinu:*
"*Avinu shebashamayim yitkadesh shmecha. Tavo malchutecha, y'aseh retzonecha ka'asher bashamayim gam be'aretz. Et lechem chukenu ten lanu hayom.*"   "Our Father who is in heaven, may your name be sanctified. May your kingdom come; as your will is done in heaven, may it also be on earth. Give us the bread that is our allotment today."

Hebrew Names & Dates from This Week:

Moshe = Moses   *Mishkan = Tabernacle*
- - - - - - - - - -
Today's story took place at the base of Mount Sinai in ~1446 BCE.

—Tetzaveh—

Exodus 27:20-30:10 | Instructions for the Priests

Yeshua is Our High Priest

This week we learned about the priesthood that God set up to be in charge of His worship. The role of the priest was very important in God's design for Israel. The priests were responsible for three main things: Service to God, Teaching the people, and Prayer. We also learned that Yeshua is our Messiah and our High Priest!

I've learned my Memory Verse!

Simple

"We may receive mercy and find grace for help in time of need." *Hebrews 4:16b*

Complete

"For we do not have a high priest (*kohen gadol*) who is unable to sympathize with our weaknesses, but One who has been tempted in all the same ways—yet without sin. Therefore let us draw near to the throne of grace with boldness, so that we may receive mercy and find grace for help in time of need." *Hebrews 4:15-16*

____

Teacher/Parent's Signature

I'm Practicing Godly Character!

This week we learned about **Encouragement**. Encouragement is when we use our words to spur someone on to doing what is right.

Here's how I practiced encouragement this week:

____

____

____

We reviewed our past four new Hebrew phrases:

ma shlomcha/shlomech?　מַה שְׁלוֹמְךָ　How are you?

tov me'od　טוֹב מְאֹד　very good

ani sameach/smechah　אֲנִי שָׂמֵחַ　I'm happy

ani atzuv/atzuvah　אֲנִי עָצוּב　I'm sad

And we reviewed the last part of the *Avinu*:

"*U'mechal lanu al chovoteinu, ka-asher machalnu gam anachnu lechayaveinu. V'al t'viyeinu lidei nisayon ki im tachaltzeinu min hara.*"　"Pardon us our debts as we also have pardoned those indebted to us. Do not bring us into the hands of testing, but rescue us from what is evil."

Hebrew Names & Dates from This Week:

Moshe = Moses　　Yeshua = Jesus
kohen gadol = high priest
kohen = priest　　Mishkan = Tabernacle

- - - - - - - - - -

Today's story took place at the base of Mount Sinai in ~1446 BCE.

–Ki Tisa–

Exodus 30:11-34:35 | The Golden Calf

God is Full of Mercy

This week we learned that while Moshe was on Mount Sinai receiving the Torah from God, the people were creating a golden calf to worship instead of God. When Moses found out, he broke the tablets of God's words and destroyed the golden calf. However, he also asked God to forgive the people, which God did because of His great mercy for us!

I've learned my Memory Verse!

SIMPLE

"ADONAI, the compassionate and gracious God, slow to anger, and abundant in lovingkindness..." *Exodus 34:6b*

COMPLETE

"Then ADONAI passed before him, and proclaimed, 'ADONAI, ADONAI, the compassionate and gracious God, slow to anger, and abundant in lovingkindness and truth, showing mercy to a thousand generations, forgiving iniquity and transgression and sin.'" *Exodus 34:6-7a*

____

Teacher/Parent's Signature

I'm Practicing Godly Character!

This week we learned about **Mercy**.
Mercy is forgiving and not punishing
someone when they do wrong to you.

Here's how I practiced mercy this week:

____

____

____

We learned a new Hebrew word:

Is it possible? (Like "May I?")

efshar   אֶפְשָׁר   (ehf-SHAR)

And we reviewed the *Avinu* in Hebrew:

*"Avinu shebashamayim yitkadesh shmecha. Tavo malchu-
techa, y'aseh retzonecha ka'asher bashamayim gam b'aretz.
Et lechem chukenu ten lanu hayom. U'mechal lanu al chovoteinu, ka-asher machalnu gam anachnu lechayaveinu. V'al
t'viyeinu lidei nisayon ki im tachaltzeinu min hara. Ki lecha
hamamlecha v'hagevurah v'hatif'eret l'olmei olamim. Amen."*

Hebrew Names & Dates from This Week:

Moshe = Moses   Aharon = Aaron

- - - - - - - - - -

Today's story took place at the base of Mount
Sinai in ~1446 BCE.

–Vayachel/Pekudei–

Exodus 35:4-40:38 | Building the Tabernacle

God Wants to Dwell with Us

This week we learned that after the golden calf incident, Moshe went back up Mount Sinai where God gave him a new set of tablets with His instruction. Then Moses led the people in creating the beautiful Tabernacle that God designed! Everyone gave of their best posessions and skills to make a beautiful place for God to dwell!

I've Learned My Memory Verse!

SIMPLE

"ADONAI your God is with you wherever you go." *Joshua 1:9b*

COMPLETE

"Have I not commanded you? Chazak! Be strong! Do not be terrified or dismayed, for ADONAI your God is with you wherever you go." *Joshua 1:9*

____

Teacher/Parent's Signature

I'm Practicing Godly Character!

This week we learned about **Generosity**. Generosity means being willing to give or share. It's the opposite of being stingy.

Here's how I practiced generosity this week:

____

____

____

We learned a new Hebrew phrase:

May we/I play?

efshar lesachek אֶפְשָׁר לְשַׂחֵק (ehf-SHAR leh-sah-CHEK)

And we reviewed the *Avinu* in English:

"Our Father who is in heaven, may your name be sanctified. May your kingdom come; as your will is done in heaven, may it also be on earth. Give us the bread that is our allotment today. Pardon us our debts as we also have pardoned those indebted to us. Do not bring us into the hands of testing, but rescue us from what is evil. For yours is the kingdom and the power and the majesty, forever and ever. Amen.

Hebrew Names & Dates from This Week:

Moshe = Moses   Aharon = Aaron
Mishkan=Tabernacle

- - - - - - - - - -

Today's story took place at the base of Mount Sinai in ~1445 BCE.

Unit 3: Vayikra | Leviticus

Welcome to your third unit of Adventures in the Torah! We hope you had fun learning about the Exodus from Egypt and the Israelites' first months in the wilderness in Exodus. God used the events of Exodus to free His people from slavery to a pagan (not godly) power in order for them to belong to and worship Him alone.

The third book of the Torah is Leviticus, or in Hebrew, *Vayikra*. That's pronounced *vah-yee-**krah***. *Vayikra* means "And He called". In this book, you'll find most of the rules about how God wanted His chosen people to live for and worship Him.

The stories in Exodus give us a glimpse into Moses' childhood and young adulthood, but they mostly happened the year Moses was 80. The rules in Leviticus are all mostly given to Moshe during his 40 days on Mount Sinai. We'll learn about the next 40 years of wandering in the wilderness in the next unit - Numbers!

A Closer look at the Exodus & Wandering:

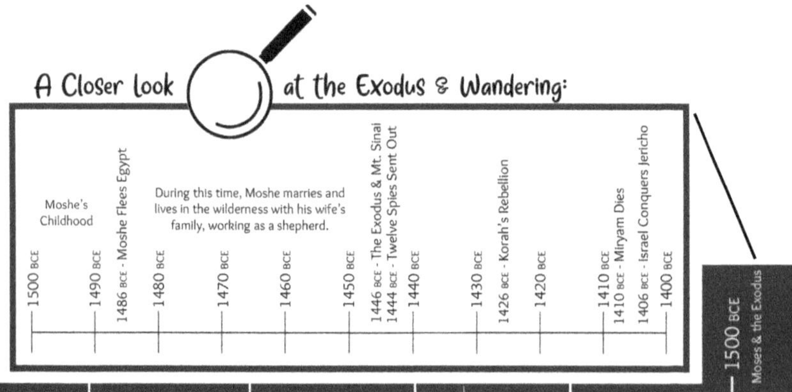

During this unit you will also learn the prayers that are recited in most synagogues when the Torah scroll is open. The Torah is a big part of our worship in Messianic Judaism because we love God's word!

You'll also learn some commonly-used Hebrew words and memorize lots of verses from Scripture. Let's go!

Main Characters of Leviticus:

God {HaShem} - Our Father in Heaven is the main character of all of Scripture. In Leviticus, He gives His people the structure for worshiping Him, which is very important!

Moses - Moses (Moshe) was the man God used to free the Hebrews from slavery and lead them in the wilderness

Tabernacle/*Mishkan* - one of the biggest "characters" of Leviticus is the worship service to HaShem, which would take place in the Tabernacle

High Priest/Priesthood - God set the men in Aaron's family line to be priests in the Tabernacle, one to serve as high priest in each generation

Sacrifices - things dedicated to God, either burned, given to the priests, or eaten in celebration for things God has done

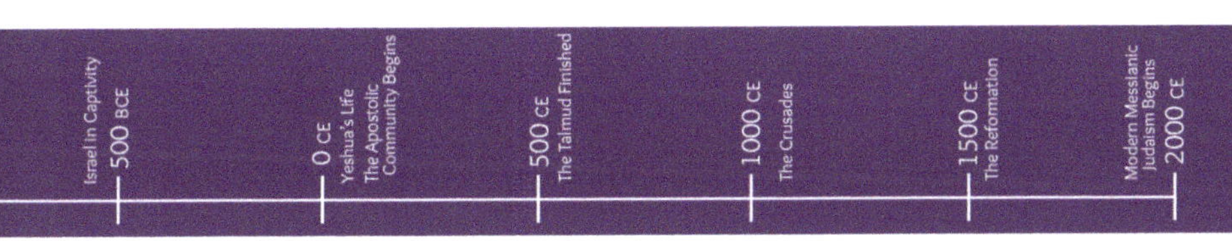

–Vayikra–

Leviticus 1:1-5:26(6:7) | The Sacrifices

God Wants Us to Draw Close

This week we read that there were 5 kinds of sacrifices - each with its own purpose. While the daily burnt offering was given completely to God, there were offerings that were given to the priests, and others that were dedicated to God and then eaten in celebration with family and friends! The point of all of the sacrifices was to draw close to God, which is what He wants most!

I've Learned My Memory Verse!

SIMPLE

"We have been made holy through the offering of the body of Messiah Yeshua."
Hebrews 10:10

COMPLETE

"By His will we have been made holy through the offering of the body of Messiah Yeshua once for all... For by one offering He has perfected forever those being made holy." *Hebrews 10:10, 14*

____

Teacher/Parent's Signature

I'm Practicing Godly Character!

This week we learned about **Confidence**. Confidence means being sure of yourself and your abilities.

Here's how I practiced confidence this week:

____

____

____

We learned a new Hebrew phrase:

May we/I talk?

efshar ledaber אֶפְשָׁר לְדַבֵּר (ehf-SHAR leh-dah-BEHR)

And we began learning the blessing we say when we open the Torah scroll in our services. This line is said by the chazzan or leader:

(Leader) "*Barchu et Adonai ham vorach.*"

(Leader) "Bless the Lord, the Blessed One"

Hebrew Names & Dates from This Week:

olah = burnt offering   *minchah = grain offering*
shelem = peace offering   *chatat = sin offering*
asham = guilt offering

- - - - - - - - - -

Today's story took place at the base of Mount Sinai in ~1445 BCE.

–Tzav–

Leviticus 6:1(8)-8:36 | Making Things Right

God Wants Us to Right Our Wrongs

This week we talked about making things right when we wrong someone. We read that God tells us that when we realize we did something wrong to someone and feel bad about it, we need to make things right by apologizing, and then doing something to make it right for that person. God wants us to live at peace with each other!

I've Learned My Memory Verse!

SIMPLE

"Do to others what you would want them to do to you." *Matthew 7:12a*

COMPLETE

"So in all things, do to others what you would want them to do to you—for this is the Torah and the Prophets." *Matthew 7:12*

- THIS IS CALLED THE "GOLDEN RULE!" -

____

Teacher/Parent's Signature

I'm Practicing Godly Character!

This week we learned about **Sincerity**. Sincerity means being real and not fake in your heart towards others.

Here's how I practiced sincerity this week:

____

____

____

We learned a new Hebrew phrase:

May I go to the bathroom?

efshar lalechet lashirutim   (lah-LECH-et lah-shee-roo-TEEM)

אֶפְשָׁר לָלֶכֶת לָשִׁירוּתִים

And we continued learning the Torah blessings. This is what the congregation says in response to what we learned last week:

(*Everyone*) "Baruch Adonai ham vorach le'olam va'ed."
(*Everyone*) "Blessed is the Lord, the Blessed One for all eternity."

Hebrew Names & Dates from This Week:

no Hebrew names

- - - - - - - - - -

Today's story took place at the base of Mount Sinai in ~1445 BCE.

Hebrew & Liturgy Review

–Shemini–

Leviticus 9:1-11:47 | Kosher Laws

God Cares About What We Eat

This week we learned that God set rules for what His people were allowed to eat. Whether it lived on land, sea, or air, God said that there were only certain animals to be eaten.

This was because His people were to be set apart from the nations around them, even in how they ate!

I've learned my Memory Verse!

Simple

"Present your bodies as a living sacrifice—holy, acceptable to God."
Romans 12:1 (selection)

Complete

"I urge you therefore, brothers and sisters, by the mercies of God, to present your bodies as a living sacrifice—holy, acceptable to God—which is your spiritual service." *Romans 12:1*

____

Teacher/Parent's Signature

I'm Practicing Godly Character!

This week we learned about **Self-Control**.
Self-control means just what it sounds like -
choosing to control yourself.

Here's how I practiced self-control this week:

____

____

____

We reviewed our last four Hebrew phrases:

efshar chatif? אֶפְשָׁר חָטִיף (May we have a snack)

efshar lesachek? אֶפְשָׁר לְשַׂחֵק (May we play?)

efshar ledaber? אֶפְשָׁר לְדַבֵּר (May we talk?)

efshar lalechet lashirutim? אֶפְשָׁר לָלֶכֶת לְשִׁירוּתִים
(May I go to the bathroom?)

And we continued learning the Torah blessings. The next blessing is that the cantor/chazzan or leader repeats what we learned last week.

HEBREW NAMES & DATES FROM THIS WEEK:

kashrut = kosher (clean and fit for eating)

Today's story took place at the base of Mount Sinai in ~1445 BCE.

-Tazria/Metzora-

Leviticus 12:1-15:33 | Leprosy/Uncleanness

God Wants Us to Speak Well About Others

This week we learned about the biblical disease of leprosy. We talked about how it could affect houses as well as people. If someone had leprosy, they couldn't live with everyone else. We also learned that scholars believe leprosy was a punishment for unkind speech about others. Our choices of words are important to God!

I've Learned My Memory Verse!

SIMPLE

"Let no harmful word come out of your mouth." *Ephesians 4:29a*

COMPLETE

"Let no harmful word come out of your mouth, but only what is beneficial for building others up according to the need, so that it gives grace to those who hear it." *Ephesians 4:29*

____
Teacher/Parent's Signature

I'm Practicing Godly Character!

This week we learned about **Honor**.
Honor means treating others with respect and admiration.

Here's how I practiced honor this week:

____

____

____

HEBREW NAMES & DATES FROM THIS WEEK:

tza'arat = biblical leprosy (different from the modern sickness we know of now)
lashan hara = evil speech (about someone)

- - - - - - - - - -

Today's story took place at the base of Mount Sinai in ~1445 BCE.

—Acharei Mot/Kedoshim—

Leviticus 16:1-20:27 | Yom Kippur/Holiness

God Calls Us to Be Holy

This week we learned about the ceremony of Yom Kippur, the Day of Atonement. On this day, the high priest did some specific things to atone for the national sin of Israel. We learned that to atone for sin is to make things right and remove the guilt of the sin, and we also learned that this is what Messiah Yeshua does for us so that we can be holy before HIm!

I've learned my Memory Verse!

Simple

"Be holy yourselves in everything you do." *1 Peter 1:15b*

Complete

"Just like the Holy One who called you, be holy yourselves also in everything you do. For it is written, '*Kedoshim* you shall be, for I am *kadosh*.'" *1 Peter 1:15-16*

____

Teacher/Parent's Signature

I'm Practicing Godly Character!

This week we learned about **Discernment**. Discernment means recognizing what is right and wrong so you can choose what is right.

Here's how I practiced discernment this week:

____

____

____

We learned to say a new Hebrew phrase:

I'm sorry / Excuse me

slicha!   (slee-CHAH)

סְלִיחָה

And we learned the last part of the blessing recited before the reading of the Torah:

(*Leader*) "*Baruch atah* Adonai, *notein ha Torah.*"
(*Everyone*) "Amen."

(*Leader*) "Blessed are You, O Lord, giver of the Torah." (*Everyone*) "Amen."

Hebrew Names & Dates from This Week:

kohen gadol = high priest
Yeshua = Jesus

- - - - - - - - - -

Today's story took place at the base of Mount Sinai in ~1445 BCE.

–Emor–

Leviticus 21:1-24:23 | Biblical Holidays
God Created Special Days

This week we learned about the weekly Sabbath day and the seven yearly feasts that God created for His people to celebrate!

We learned that there are 3 things God told Israel to do on those days: 1. Rest from regular work, 2. Meet with God, 3. Gather with others. By doing these things, we get to celebrate God's way!

I've learned my Memory Verse!

SIMPLE

"The seventh day is a Shabbat of solemn rest." *Leviticus 23:3* (selection)

COMPLETE

"Work may be done for six days, but the seventh day is a Shabbat of solemn rest, a holy convocation. You are to do no work—it is a Shabbat to Adonai in all your dwellings." *Leviticus 23:3*

____

Teacher/Parent's Signature

I'm Practicing Godly Character!

This week we learned about **Attentiveness**.
Attentiveness means paying attention to
what is happening around us.

Here's how I practiced attentiveness this week:

____

____

____

We learned a new Hebrew word:

Stop!

tafsik! תַּפְסִיק (tahf-SEEK) - to a boy

tafsiki (tahf-SEE-kee) - to a girl | *tafsiku* (*koo) - to a group

And we learned the first part of the blessing the
cantor/leader recites when the Torah scroll is closed:

"*Baruch atah Adonai, Eloheinu Melech ha'olam, asher natan
lanu Toraht emet, ve'ha'yay olam natah b'tocheynu.*"

"Blessed are You, O Lord our God, King of the universe,
who gave us the Torah of truth and planted everlasting
life within us."

Hebrew Names & Dates from This Week:

Shabbat = Sabbath
*We also went through each of the holidays today - more
info can be found in the holiday lessons*

- - - - - - - - - -

*Today's story took place at the base of Mount
Sinai in ~1445 BCE.*

-Behar/Bechukotai-

Leviticus 25:1-27:34 | The Finale on Mt. Sinai

God Rewards Us for Our Obedience

We finished Leviticus learning about the rest and jubilee years that God told His people to keep. Every 7 years they were to give the land rest, and every 50th year land would go back to its original owner. God promised that if they obeyed Him in this, He'd provide lots of blessings to provide for them and give them rest!

I've Learned My Memory Verse!

SIMPLE

"I will be your God, and you will be My people." *Leviticus 26:12b*

COMPLETE

"I will set My Tabernacle among you, and My soul will not abhor you. I will walk among you and will be your God, and you will be My people." *Leviticus 26:11-12*

____

Teacher/Parent's Signature

I'm Practicing Godly Character!

This week we learned about **Initiative**.
Initiative is when we are willing to get things done and take responsibility.

Here's how I practiced initiative this week:

____

____

____

We learned a new Hebrew phrase:

Have a good week!

shavua tov!   (shah-VOO-ah TOHV)

שָׁבוּעַ טוֹב

And we learned the rest of the blessing the cantor/ leader recites when the Torah scroll is closed:

"*Baruch atah Adonai, notein haTorah. Amen.*"

"Blessed are You, O Lord, giver of the Torah. Amen."

Hebrew Names & Dates from This Week:

shemitah = rest year every seven years
yovel = jubilee year every fifty years

- - - - - - - - - -

Today's story took place at the base of Mount Sinai in ~1445 BCE.

Unit 4: Bamidbar | Numbers

Welcome to your fourth unit of Adventures in the Torah! We hope you had fun learning about the rules God gave His people in Leviticus. While we might think of rules as boring, God's rules are perfect, and they give us a look into His heart of love for His people.

The fourth book of the Torah is Numbers, or in Hebrew, *Bamidbar*. That's pronounced *bah-meed-***bar***. Bamidbar* means "In the wilderness". In this book, you'll find the adventures of God's people in the 40 years they spent wandering the wilderness between Mount Sinai and the Promised Land.

During these 40 years, God teaches the Israelites a lot about Himself, protects them from the surrounding nations, and provides their every need. There's quite a bit of drama, but also lots of simple hot days in the sun!

During this unit you will also learn the blessings we say when we begin *Shabbat* every Friday night with the traditional candles, *challah* bread, and grape juice!

You'll also learn some commonly-used Hebrew words and memorize lots of verses from Scripture. Let's go!

Main Characters of Numbers:

The book of Numbers is continuation of the previous books, so there aren't any new major characters. We do get to meet a lot of interesting people, like Joshua (who will be a major character later in the Bible), Caleb, Balaam, Korach, and the 5 daughters of Zelophehad.

–Bamidbar–

Numbers 1:1-4:20 | Arranging the Camp
God Designed Families

This week we began the book of Numbers by learning how God organized the camp of Israel. We talked about how God set aside the tribe of Levi to serve Him at the Tabernacle instead of the firstborn from every family. This helped keep families together and shows us that God loves families!

I've Learned My Memory Verse!

SIMPLE

"It is good for brothers (and sisters) to live in unity! *Psalm 133:1*
(author's paraphrase)

COMPLETE

"Behold, how good and how pleasant it is for brothers (and sisters) to dwell together in unity!" *Psalm 133:1*

____
Teacher/Parent's Signature

I'm Practicing Godly Character!

This week we learned about **Loyalty**. Loyalty means being there for someone through the good times and bad times.

Here's how I practiced loyalty this week:

____

____

We reviewed our last four Hebrew phrases:

atah/at beseder? אַתָּה/אַת בְּסֵדֶר (Are you okay?)

ani beseder! אֲנִי בְּסֵדֶר (I'm okay!)

slicha! סְלִיחָה (I'm sorry/Excuse me!)

tafsik/i/u! תַּפְסִיק (Stop! *to a boy/girl/group*)

shavua tov! שָׁבוּעַ טוֹב (Have a good week!)

And we started learning the Erev Shabbat blessings. The first one is the blessing for lighting the candles:

"Baruch atah Adonai, Eloheinu Melech ha'olam, asher kid'shanu b'mitzvotav v'tzivanu l'hadlik ner shel Shabbat."

Hebrew Names & Dates from This Week:

no Hebrew names

- - - - - - - - - -

Today's story took place at the base of Mount Sinai in ~1445 BCE.

–Nasso–

Numbers 4:21-7:89 | The Aaronic Blessing
We Belong to God

This week we learned about two things - the Nazirite vow and the Aaronic blessing. The Nazirite vow was a special way people could dedicate themselves to God for a period of time, and the Aaronic blessing was something the priests would pray over the people. God said that this blessing (below) was how His name was placed on His people!

I've learned my Memory Verse!

SIMPLE

"The Lord bless you and keep you."
Numbers 6:24

COMPLETE

"The Lord bless you and keep you; The Lord make his face to shine upon you and be gracious to you; The Lord lift up his countenance upon you and give you peace." *Numbers 6:24-26*

____

Teacher/Parent's Signature

I'm Practicing Godly Character!

This week we learned about **Creativity**.
Creativity means being able to use your thoughts or imagination to create.

Here's how I practiced creativity this week:

____

____

____

We learned a new Hebrew word:

Friend (boy): *chaver* חֶבֵר (cha-VEHR)

Friend (girl): *chaverah* חֲבֵרָה (cha-veh-RAH)

And we learned the English for the candlelighting blessing said on Erev Shabbat:

"Blessed are You, O LORD our God, King of the universe, who has sanctified us with His commandments and commanded us to kindle the Sabbath lights."

HEBREW NAMES & DATES FROM THIS WEEK:

no Hebrew names

- - - - - - - - - -

Today's story took place at the base of Mount Sinai in ~1445 BCE.

– Beha'alotcha –

Numbers 8:1-12:16 | Rebellious Attitudes

God Knows What's Best for Us

Today we talked about a few episodes that happened when God's people had bad attitudes. The people complained about being in the desert and not having meat, and then Aaron & Miryam complained about Moses! In all of these, God punished them for not trusting in Him. We need to trust that God knows best!

I've learned my Memory Verse!

Simple

"My thoughts are not your thoughts, nor are your ways My ways." *Isaiah 55:8*

Complete

"'For My thoughts are not your thoughts, nor are your ways My ways.' It is a declaration of Adonai. 'For as the heavens are higher than earth, so are My ways higher than your ways, and My thoughts than your thoughts.'" *Isaiah 55:8-9*

____

Teacher/Parent's Signature

I'm Practicing Godly Character!

This week we learned about **Resourcefulness**. Resourcefulness means being able to handle challenges by figuring things out.

Here's how I practiced resourcefulness this week:

____

____

____

We learned two new Hebrew words:

Brother: *ach* אָח (ACH)

Sister: *achot* אָחוֹת (ah-CHOT)

And we learned the first part of an alternate candle-lighting blessing often used by Messianic families:

"Baruch atah Adonai, Eloheinu Melech ha'olam, asher kid'shanu b'mitzvotav v'tzivanu liheyot or lagoyim…"

"Blessed are You, O Lord our God, King of the universe, who has sanctified us with His commandments and commanded us to be a light to the nations…

Hebrew Names & Dates from This Week:

Aharon = Aaron　　　*Miryam = Miriam*

Mishkan = Tabernacle

- - - - - - - - - -

Today's story took place in the wilderness of Paran in ~1445 bce.

–Shelach–

Numbers 13:1-15:41 | The 12 Spies

We Should be Careful Who We Listen To

Lesson 33

We've come to the story of the 12 spies! We learned that they saw how good the Promised Land was but also how hard it would be to conquer. Instead of trusting in God's strength to help them, all but Joshua and Caleb said that they shouldn't even try. As a punishment, God gave His People 40 years of wandering the wilderness!

I've learned my Memory Verse!

Simple

"Bad company corrupts good morals."
1 Corinthians 15:33

Complete

"Do not be deceived! Bad company corrupts good morals."
1 Corinthians 15:33

____
Teacher/Parent's Signature

I'm Practicing Godly Character!

This week we learned about **Leadership**. Leadership means living your life in a way that others want to follow you.

Here's how I practiced leadership this week:

____

____

____

We learned to say two new Hebrew words:

Dad: *abba*   אַבָּא   (AH-bah)

Mom: *imma*   אִמָּא   (EE-mah)

And we learned the last part of the alternate candle-lighting blessing:

"…v'natan lanu et Yeshua meshicheinu or ha'olam."

"… and has given us Yeshua our Messiah, the light of the world."

Hebrew Names & Dates from This Week:

Calev = Caleb

Yehoshua = Joshua

- - - - - - - - - -

Today's story took place just outside the Promised Land - Canaan - in ~1445 BCE.

–Korach–

Numbers 16:1-18:32 | Korah's Rebellion

God Cares About Our Attitudes

This week we read two intense stories that teach us how important our attitudes are! In the first one, a man named Korach organized a rebellion against Moses and was swallowed by the ground. Then, God sent a plague on the people for grumbling against Moses, and Aaron had to stop it by running into the people with a censor full of incense! Our attitudes matter to God!

I've learned my Memory Verse!

SIMPLE

"Do everything without grumbling or arguing." *Philippians 2:14a*

COMPLETE

"Do everything without grumbling or arguing, so that you might be blameless and innocent, children of God in the midst of a crooked and twisted generation. Among them you shine as lights in the world." *Philippians 2:14-15*

____

Teacher/Parent's Signature

I'm Practicing Godly Character!

This week we learned about **Humility**.
Humility means thinking less about yourself
and more about others.

Here's how I practiced humility this week:

____

____

____

Hebrew & Liturgy Review

We learned a new Hebrew word:

Teacher (boy): *moreh* מוֹרֶה (mo-REH)

Teacher (girl): *morah* מוֹרָה (mo-RAH)

And we learned *Kiddush* - the blessing recited when
we drink wine/grape juice on Erev Shabbat:

*"Baruch atah Adonai, Eloheinu Melech ha'olam, borei
p'ri hagafen."*

"Blessed are You, O Lord our God, King of the
universe, creator of the fruit of the vine."

Hebrew Names & Dates from This Week:

Moshe = Moses　　　*Aharon = Aaron*
Korach = Korah

- - - - - - - - - -

*Today's story took place just outside the Promised
Land (Canaan) in ~1444 BCE.*

–Chukat/Balak–

Numbers 19:1-25:9 | Balaam & His Donkey

God Cares About Our Words

This week we learned about the false prophet named Balaam and his talking donkey. One of Israel's enemies' kings paid Balaam to curse Israel, but whenever he opened his mouth, only blessing came out. We learned that God cares about the words that we use and wants us to use only words that build others up!

I've Learned My Memory Verse!

SIMPLE

"Death and life are in the control of the tongue." *Proverbs 18:21a*

COMPLETE

"Death and life are in the control of the tongue. Those who indulge in it will eat its fruit." *Proverbs 18:21*

____

Teacher/Parent's Signature

I'm Practicing Godly Character!

This week we learned about **Tactfulness**. Tactfulness or having tact means the ability to deal with others without offending them.

Here's how I practiced tactfulness this week:

____

____

We reviewed our last four Hebrew words:

chaver/chaverah חָבֵר / חֲבֵרָה (friend boy/girl)

ach/achot אָח / אָחוֹת (brother/sister)

abba/imma אַבָּא / אִמָּא (dad/mom)

moreh/morah מוֹרֶה / מוֹרָה (teacher man/woman)

And we read the longer part of the Kiddush blessing:

"Blessed are You, O Lord our God, King of the universe, who has sanctified us with His commandments, and chosen us, and given us in love and favor His holy Shabbat as an inheritance, as a remembrance of the act of creation. For this day is the beginning of all holy days, a remembrance of the Exodus from Egypt. You have chosen us and have blessed us from among all the nations, and with love and favor You have given us Your holy Shabbat. Blessed are You, O Lord, who sanctifies Shabbat."

Hebrew Names & Dates from This Week:

no Hebrew names

- - - - - - - - - -

Today's story took place at Kadesh Barnea in ~1408 BCE.

Are my words...

T - True

H - Helpful

I - Inspiring

N - Necessary

K - Kind   ?

–Pinchas–

Numbers 25:10-30:1 (29:40) | Joshua is Commissioned

We Should be Good Stewards

This week we learned about five sisters who protected their father's inheritance in Israel, asking to have it pass on to them since they didn't have a brother. We also learned about Moshe anointing Joshua as the next leader of Israel. In both of these stories, we saw how God wants us to care for what He has entrusted to us!

I've learned My Memory Verse!

Simple

"Whatever you do, work at it from the soul." *Colossians 3:23a*

Complete

"Whatever you do, work at it from the soul, as for the Lord and not for people. For you know that from the Lord you will receive the inheritance as a reward." *Colossians 3:23-24*

____

Teacher/Parent's Signature

I'm Practicing Godly Character!

This week we learned about **Stewardship**. Stewardship means knowing that all we have belongs to God, and taking good care of it.

Here's how I practiced stewardship this week:

____

____

____

We started learning how to count in Hebrew:

One: *achat*   אַחַת   (ah-CHAT)

Two: *shtaim*   שְׁתַּיִם   (SHTAH-yeem)

Three: *shalosh*   שָׁלֹשׁ   (shah-LOSH)

And we learned the *HaMotzi* - the blessing recited before eating bread:

"Baruch atah Adonai, Eloheinu Melech ha'olam, hamotzi lechem min ha'aretz."

"Blessed are You, O Lord our God, King of the universe, who brings forth bread from the earth."

Hebrew Names & Dates from This Week:

Yehoshua = Joshua

Moshe = Moses

Today's story took place in Kadesh Barnea in ~1407 bce.

–Mattot/Massei–

Numbers 30:2(1)-36:13 | Tribes Ask for Land

We Should Keep Our Promises

We're at the end of the book of Numbers and learned that God brought His people across the Jordan River from Canaan! A few tribes saw how good the land was, and asked for that land as their inheritance instead of the land in Canaan. Moses agreed - after they promised that they would still fight with the rest of their fellow men for the Promised Land.

I've learned my Memory Verse!

SIMPLE

"Whenever a man makes a vow, he is to do everything."
Numbers 30:2a (author's paraphrase)

COMPLETE

"Whenever a man makes a vow to Adonai or swears an oath to obligate himself by a pledge, he is not to violate his word but do everything coming out of his mouth."
Numbers 30:2

____

Teacher/Parent's Signature

I'm Practicing Godly Character!

This week we learned about **Reliability**. Reliability means being dependable, being a person that others can count on.

Here's how I practiced reliability this week:

____

____

____

We continued learning how to count in Hebrew:

Four: *arba*   אַרְבַּע   (AHR-bah)

Five: *chamesh*   חָמֵשׁ   (chah-MESH)

Six: *shesh*   שֵׁשׁ   (SHESH)

And we had fun in class practicing all we've learned for having an Erev Shabbat meal at home!

Hebrew Names & Dates from This Week:

no Hebrew names

- - - - - - - - - -

Today's story took place just across the Jordan River from the Promised Land in ~1406 BCE.

Unit 5: Devarim | Deuteronomy

Welcome to your fifth unit of Adventures in the Torah! We hope you enjoyed learning about the 40 years Israel spent wandering the wilderness between Mount Sinai and the Promised Land, and all the drama that unfolded!

The last book of the Torah is Deuteronomy, or in Hebrew, *Devarim*. That's pronounced *deh-vahr-**eem***. *Devarim* means "Words". In this book, you'll find Moses' 5-week speech (with lots of words!) that he gave to the Israelites before they entered the Promised Land without him.

Remember - as a punishment for disobedience, Moses was forbidden from entering the Promised Land. But as a good leader who loved his people, Moses spend the last several weeks of his life teaching and reminding the people of all that God has done for them, and that is what we'll be studing this unit!

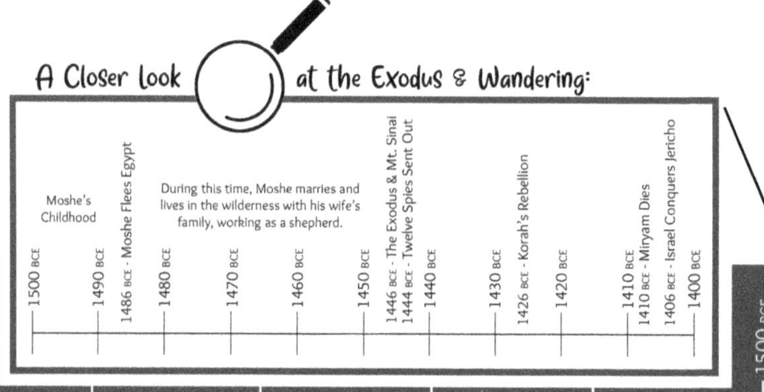

Last unit you learned the blessings that we recite as we begin our Shabbat celebration each week. During this unit you will learn the blessings for Havdalah - a special ceremony that ends Shabbat each week. As you can see, Shabbat is a big deal in Messianic Judaism!

You'll also learn some commonly-used Hebrew words and memorize lots of verses from Scripture. Let's go!

–Devarim–

Deuteronomy 1:1-3:22 | Moses Begins

We Need to Remember What God Does for Us

We began the last book of the Torah today and learned that the whole book of Deuteronomy is Moses recalling all that God had done for Israel over the past 40 years. His last major act as their leader was to remind them of God's love and care for them and encourage them to always serve Him!

I've Learned My Memory Verse!

SIMPLE

"I will remember the deeds of ADONAI."
Psalm 77:11a (12a in Jewish Scriptures)

COMPLETE

"I will remember the deeds of ADONAI. Yes, I will muse about Your wonders of old. I will meditate also on all Your work and consider Your deeds."
Psalm 77:11-12 (12-13 in Jewish Scriptures)

____

Teacher/Parent's Signature

I'm Practicing Godly Character!

This week we learned about **Perseverence**. Perseverance means continuing to work at a task until it's finished.

Here's how I practiced perseverence this week:

____

____

____

We continued learning how to count in Hebrew:

Seven: *sheva* שֶׁבַע (SHEY-vah)

Eight: *sh'moneh* שְׁמוֹנֶה (SHMOAN-ey)

Nine: *tesha* תֵּשַׁע (TEY-shah)

And we began learning the Havdalah blessings - the blessings that are recited as we close Shabbat on Saturday night. It begins with Isaiah 12:2-3:

"Behold, God is my salvation! I will trust and will not be afraid. For the Lord Adonai is my strength and my song. He also has become my salvation."

Hebrew Names & Dates from This Week:

no Hebrew names

- - - - - - - - - -

Today's story took place just across the Jordan River from the Promised Land in ~1406 BCE.

–Va'etchanan–

Deut. 3:23-7:11 | Moses Urges Against Idolatry

God Wants Our Whole Hearts

This week we learned that Moshe continued his talk to Israel by reminding them that God wants to be the only One we worship and He wants our whole hearts. Moses knew Israel would be tempted to worship idols like the nations around them and encouraged them to stay faithful to HaShem alone!

I've learned my Memory Verse!

Simple

"I praise You, O Lord my God, with my whole heart." *Psalm 86:12a*

Complete

"Teach me Your way, Adonai, that I may walk in Your truth. Give me an undivided heart to fear Your Name. I praise You, O Lord my God, with my whole heart, and glorify Your Name forever."
Psalm 86:11-12

____

Teacher/Parent's Signature

I'm Practicing Godly Character!

This week we learned about **Politeness**. Politeness means showing respect for others in manners, speech, and behavior.

Here's how I practiced politeness this week:

____

____

____

We finished learning our counting in Hebrew:

Ten: *eser*   עֶשֶׂר   (EH-ser)

a little: *k'tzat*   קְצָת   (kit-TZAHT)

a lot: *harbe*   הַרְבֵּה   (har-BEY)

And we continued learning the Havdalah blessings with the rest of the opening blessing:

"With joy you will draw water from the wells of salvation. Salvation belongs to the Lord; Your blessing is upon Your people. Selah."

HEBREW NAMES & DATES FROM THIS WEEK:

no Hebrew names

- - - - - - - - - -

Today's story took place just across the Jordan River from the Promised Land in ~1406 BCE.

-Ekev-

Deut. 7:12-11:25 | Israel is God's Land

Moses Reminds Israel of God's Care

This week we learned that God promised that He would take special care of the land of Israel - the land He was giving His people. As long as the Israelites continued to obey God faithfully, God would make sure that there was rain and the land would produce all they needed. God chose Israel to be His special land forever!

I've Learned My Memory Verse!

Simple

"Pray for the peace of Jerusalem."
Psalm 122:6a

Complete

"Pray for the peace of Jerusalem - may those who love you be at peace!
May there be shalom within your walls - quietness within your palaces."
Psalm 122:6-7

____
Teacher/Parent's Signature

I'm Practicing Godly Character!

This week we learned about **Flexibility**.
Flexibility means being able to change or meet new situations without it making you upset.

Here's how I practiced flexibility this week:

____

____

____

We reviewed all of our Hebrew number words:

1: *achat*   2: *shtaim*   3: *shalosh*   4: *arba*   5: *chamesh*
6: *shesh*   7: *sheva*   8: *sh'moneh*   9: *tesha*   10: *eser*
a little: *k'tzat*   a lot: *harbe*

And we learned the blessing for the spices that we smell during Havdalah:

"*Baruch atah ADONAI, Eloheinu Melech ha'olam, borei minei v'samim.*"

"Blessed are You, O LORD our God, King of the Universe, creator of various kinds of spices."

HEBREW NAMES & DATES FROM THIS WEEK:

no Hebrew names

Today's story took place just across the Jordan River from the Promised Land in ~1406 BCE.

-Ré'eh-

Deuteronomy 11:26-16:17 | Various Laws

We Should Care for the Needy

In this week's lesson, we talked about how God commands us to take care of those who are needy among us. We're supposed to be generous and give with glad hearts to those who need it, especially those who have no one else to help them. We learned that Yeshua told us that whoever cares for those in need cares for Him!

I've learned my Memory Verse!

SIMPLE

"Pure religion before God is to care for orphans and widows."
James 1:27a (author's paraphrase)

COMPLETE

"Pure and undefiled religion before our God and Father is this: to care for orphans and widows in their distress, and to keep oneself unstained by the world."
James 1:27

____

Teacher/Parent's Signature

I'm Practicing Godly Character!

This week we learned about **Hospitality**. Hospitality means being friendly, warm, and generous when taking care of others.

Here's how I practiced hospitality this week:

____

____

____

We learned two new Hebrew snack words:

apple: *tapuach* תַּפּוּחַ (tah-POO-ach) plural: *tapuchim*

banana: *banana* בַּנָנָה (bah-NAH-nah) plural: *bananot*

And we learned the blessing for the braided candle that we light during Havdalah:

"Baruch atah Adonai, Eloheinu Melech ha'olam, borei m'orei ha'eish."

"Blessed are You, O Lord our God, King of the Universe, creator of the lights of fire."

Hebrew Names & Dates from This Week:

no Hebrew names

- - - - - - - - - -

Today's story took place just across the Jordan River from the Promised Land in ~1406 BCE.

—Shoftim—

Deut. 16:18-21:9 | God's Rules for Leaders
God Wants Us to Lead Well

This week we learned about how God wants the leaders of His people to lead well. They aren't supposed to show favoritism or take a bribe. And when Israel eventually had a king, that king was to write a copy of the entire Torah for himself so that he would stay faithful to HaShem alone. God cares that we lead well, in whatever area of life we lead in!

I've learned my Memory Verse!

Simple

"Be an example of the faithful." 1 Timothy 4:12a *(author's paraphrase)*

Intermediate -

Complete

"Let no one look down on your youthfulness, but become an example of the faithful—in speech, in conduct, in love, in faithfulness, and in purity." 1 Timothy 4:12

____

Teacher/Parent's Signature

I'm Practicing Godly Character!

This week we learned about **Resiliance**. Resilience means being able to deal with and bounce back quickly from difficulty.

Here's how I practiced resiliance this week:

____

____

____

We learned two new Hebrew snack words:

carrot: *gezer*   גֶּזֶר (GEH-zehr) plural: *gezerim*

cracker: *kreker*   קְרְקֶר (KREH-ker) plural: *krekerim*

And we began learning the closing blessing for Havdalah, thanking God for what is holy:

"Baruch atah Adonai, Eloheinu Melech ha'olam, hamavdil bein kodesh lechol..."

"Blessed are You, O LORD our God, King of the Universe, who makes a distinction between what is holy and what is common..."

Hebrew & Liturgy Review

HEBREW NAMES & DATES FROM THIS WEEK:

no Hebrew names

- - - - - - - - - -

Today's story took place just across the Jordan River from the Promised Land in ~1406 BCE.

–Ki Tetze–

Deut. 21:10-25:19 | Various Laws

We Should Have Integrity

This week we learned about different ways we can show integrity - doing what's right even if no one knows. Some of the things we talked about were: returning things to those who lost them, caring kindly for animals, taking responsibility to keep our home safe, and keeping our promises. Most of these are things that no one would notice if we didn't do what is right - but God still sees!

I've learned My Memory Verse!

SIMPLE

"Let us not lose heart in doing good."
Galatians 6:9a

COMPLETE

"Let us not lose heart in doing good, for in due time we will reap if we don't give up. Therefore, whenever we have an opportunity, let us do good toward all - especially those who belong to the household of faith." *Galatians 6:9-10*

____

Teacher/Parent's Signature

I'm Practicing Godly Character!

This week we learned about **Impartiality**.
Impartiality means not favoring one person
more than another.

Here's how I practiced impartiality this week:

____

____

____

We learned two new Hebrew snack words:
cookie: *ugiyah* עוּגִיָּה (oo-GHEE-yah) plural: *ugiyot*
candy: *mamtuk* מַמְתָּק (mahm-TOOK) plural: *mamtukim*

And we continued learning the closing blessing
for Havdalah, recognizing the separation that God
makes between what is set apart for Himself and
what is ordinary:

"...bein or lechoshech, bein Yisrael la'amim..."

"...between light and darkness, between Israel and the
nations..."

Hebrew Names & Dates from This Week:

no Hebrew names

- - - - - - - - - -

*Today's story took place just across the Jordan
River from the Promised Land in ~1406 BCE.*

-Ki Tavo-

Deuteronomy 26:1-29:8 | Blessings & Curses

God is Our Father

In this week's lesson we learned that God promised lots of blessings for His people if they obeyed His commandments, but also lots of punishments if they disobeyed. Just like our parents give us privileges for doing what's right and punishments for doing wrong, God as our Heavenly Father wants to motivate us to do what is right so that we can live better for Him!

I've learned my Memory Verse!

Simple

"I am giving you a blessing if you obey the mitzvot of Adonai."
Deut. 11:26-27 (author's paraphrase)

Complete

"I am setting before you today a blessing and a curse - the blessing, if you listen to the mitzvot of Adonai your God that I am commanding you today, but the curse, if you do not listen to the mitzvot of Adonai your God." *Deut. 11:26-28a*

____

Teacher/Parent's Signature

I'm Practicing Godly Character!

This week we learned about **Thoughtfulness**.
Being thoughtful means giving careful
attention to the needs or desires of others.

Here's how I practiced thoughtfulness this
week:

____

____

____

We reviewed the Hebrew snack words we've learned:

apple: *tapuach/tapuchim* | banana: *banana/bananot*

carrot: *gezer/gezerim* | cracker: *kreker/krekerim*

cookie: *ugiyah/ugiyot* | candy: *mamtuk/mamtukim*

And we continued learning the closing blessing for
Havdalah:

"*...bein yom hashevi'i lesheshet yemei hama'aseh.*"

"*...between the seventh day and the six days of
creation.*"

Hebrew Names & Dates from This Week:

no Hebrew names

- - - - - - - - - -

*Today's story took place just across the Jordan
River from the Promised Land in ~1406 BCE.*

–Nitzavim/Vayelech–

LESSON 45

Deut. 29:9-31:30 | Moses Gives Final Encouragement

God Wants Us to Read His Word

This week we learned that after Moshe finished his 5-week speech to Israel, encouraging them to live for HaShem, he gave the written Torah to the leaders of Israel. He reminded them that he would not be going with them, but God would. And they would have His Torah with them forever to guide them!

I've learned my Memory Verse!

SIMPLE

"I have treasured Your word in my heart, so I might not sin against You."
Psalm 119:11

COMPLETE

"With my whole heart have I sought You - let me not stray from Your mitzvot. I have treasured Your word in my heart, so I might not sin against You."
Psalm 119:10-11

____
Teacher/Parent's Signature

I'm Practicing Godly Character!

This week we learned about **Cooperation**.
Cooperation means being able to work together with others.

Here's how I practiced cooperation this week:

____

____

We learned how to say two new Hebrew phrases:

It's hot: *ze cham*   זֶה חַם   (zeh chahm)

I'm hot: *cham li*   חַם לִי   (cham lee)

And we finished learning the final Havdalah blessing:

"Baruch atah Adonai, hamavdil bein kodesh lechol,"

"Blessed are You, O Lord, who makes a distinction between what is holy and what is common."

Hebrew Names & Dates from This Week:

no Hebrew names

- - - - - - - - - -

Today's story took place just across the Jordan River from the Promised Land in ~1406 BCE.

–Ha'azinu–

Deut. 32:1-52 | The Song of Moses

Music is a Great Way to Worship God

This week we read part of the Song of Moses and learned that one of Moshe's last acts as Israel's leader was to teach them a song that would remind them of God's goodness and faithfulness. We learned that God created music and wants us to use music to worship Him and remember His words!

I've learned My Memory Verse!

SIMPLE

"O come, let us sing for joy to ADONAI."
Psalm 95:1a

COMPLETE

"O come, let us sing for joy to ADONAI. Let us shout for joy to the rock of our salvation. Let us come before His presence with thanksgiving. Let us shout joyfully to Him with songs. For ADONAI is a great God and a great King above all gods." *Psalm 95:1-3*

____

Teacher/Parent's Signature

I'm Practicing Godly Character!

This week we learned about **Gentleness**. Gentleness means not being harsh - either with our bodies, or our words and attitudes.

Here's how I practiced gentleness this week:

____

____

____

We learned how to say two new Hebrew phrases:

It's cold: *ze kar*   זֶה קַר   (zeh kar)

I'm cold: *kar li*   קַר לִי   (kar lee)

And we reviewed all of the Havdalah blessings we learned these past few weeks!

Hebrew Names & Dates from This Week:

no Hebrew names

- - - - - - - - - -

Today's story took place just across the Jordan River from the Promised Land in ~1406 BCE.

-Vezot HaBracha-

Deuteronomy 33:1-34:12 | Moses' Final Blessings to Each Tribe

We Were Created for Unity

We finished the Torah this week by remembering that God created us all unique and special, and also created us to be in unity and community with each other! Just as each tribe in Israel had a unique role, God has a special place for each of His children - including you!

I've learned my Memory Verse!

You have done such an amazing job learning God's word this year!

Over the course of this year, you have memorized lots of passages of Scripture, plus gained understanding of how to apply the Torah to your life - something that will help you for a very long time to come!

We're so proud of you!

I'm Practicing Godly Character!

This week we talked about all the character traits we've grown in this year. Can you think of some ways you've grown in character this past year?

____

____

____

As we wrap up this year of study, remember that you are made special by a God who loves you very much. He has a plan for your life and a purpose for you that He is going to continue to show you as you grow in Him.

We are excited to see how you continue learning about God by reading His word, praying to Him, and staying in community with other kids and adults who love God too!

Shanah Tovah!

Happy New Year!

The Biblical Holiday Calendar

God gave us a calendar of holidays in Leviticus 23 (in the parsha *Emor*). We learned in that lesson that there are 3 things God told Israel to do on those days:

1. Rest from regular work,
2. Meet with God,
3. Gather with others.

By doing these things, we get to celebrate God's way!

Here's a list of the holidays given to us by God:

Pesach (Passover)

Matzot (Unleavened Bread)

Shavuot (Weeks)

Yom Teruah/Rosh HaShanah (Trumpets)

Yom Kippur (Day of Atonement)

Sukkot (Tabernacles)

Shemini Atzeret (The 8th Day)

There are also some days on the calendar that people created for special reasons, like Chanukah & Purim.

THE SHEHECHIYANU

The *Shehechiyanu* is a prayer said to celebrate special occasions. It expresses gratitude to God for new and special experiences as well as holidays.

בָּרוּךְ אַתָּה יְיָ אֱלֹהֵינוּ מֶלֶךְ הָעוֹלָם, שֶׁהֶחֱיָינוּ וְקִיְּמָנוּ וְהִגִּיעָנוּ לַזְּמָן הַזֶּה

Baruch atah Adonai, Eloheinu Melech ha'olam, shehechiyanu, v'kiy'manu, v'higianu lazman hazeh.

Blessed are You, O Lord our God, King of the universe, who has created us, sustained us, and enabled us to reach this season.
(Amen)

Hopefully this graphic will help you better understand how the biblical holidays fit in the year!

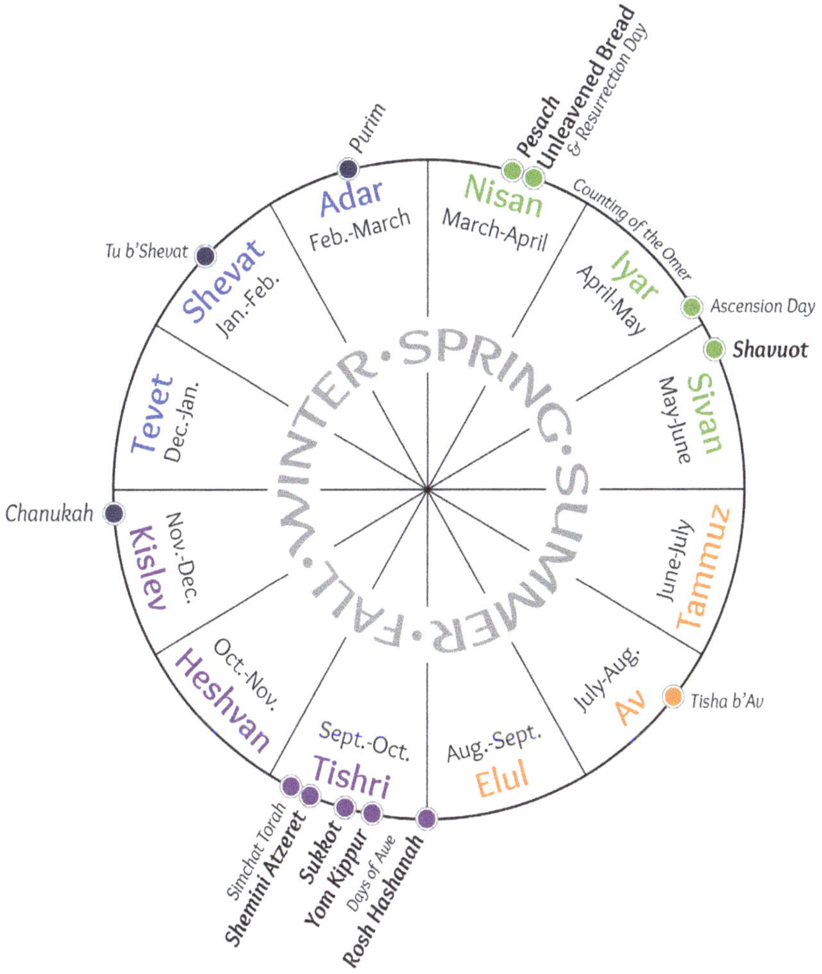

Copyright 2023 Messianic Kids

Avraham's Journeys

The Exodus & Wandering

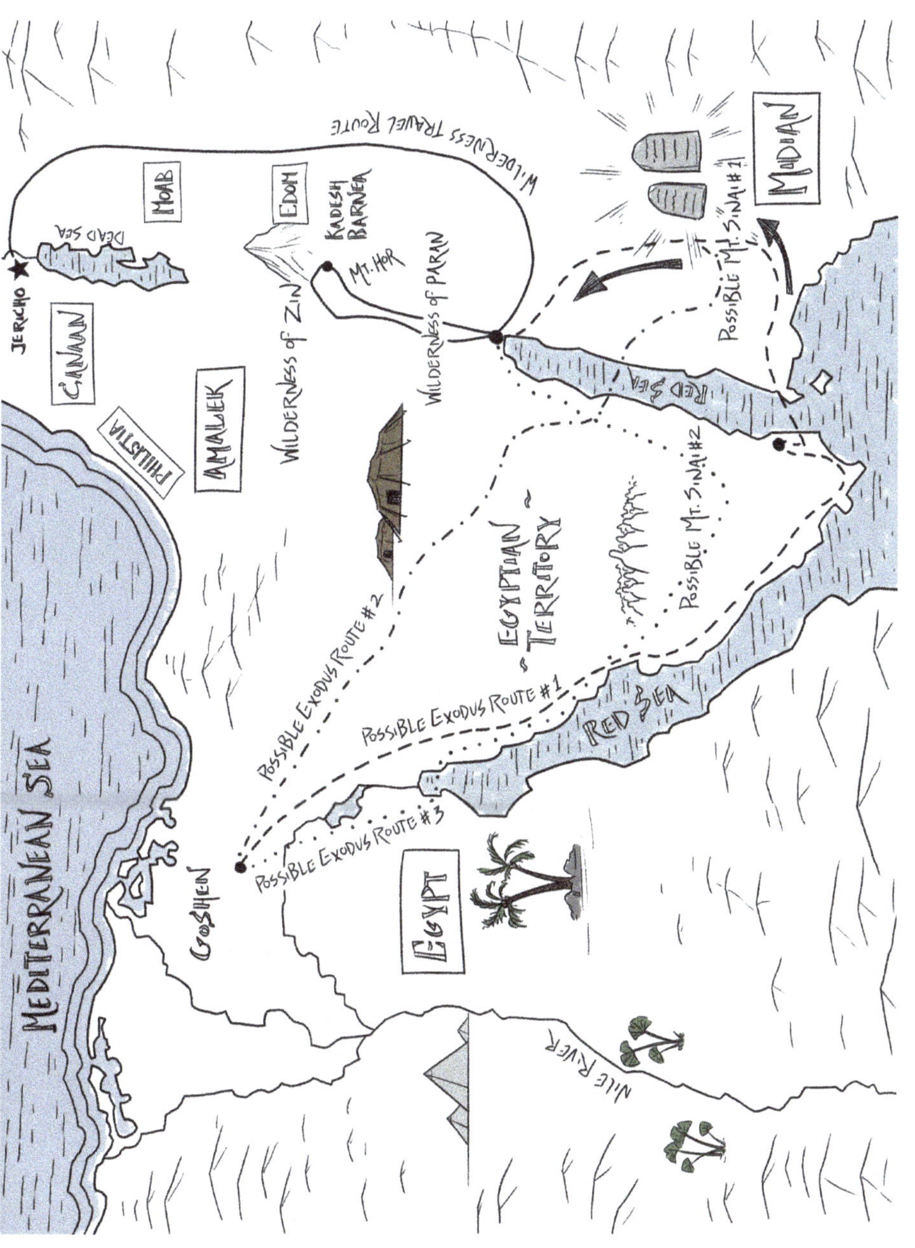

The Land of Israel Divided by Tribe

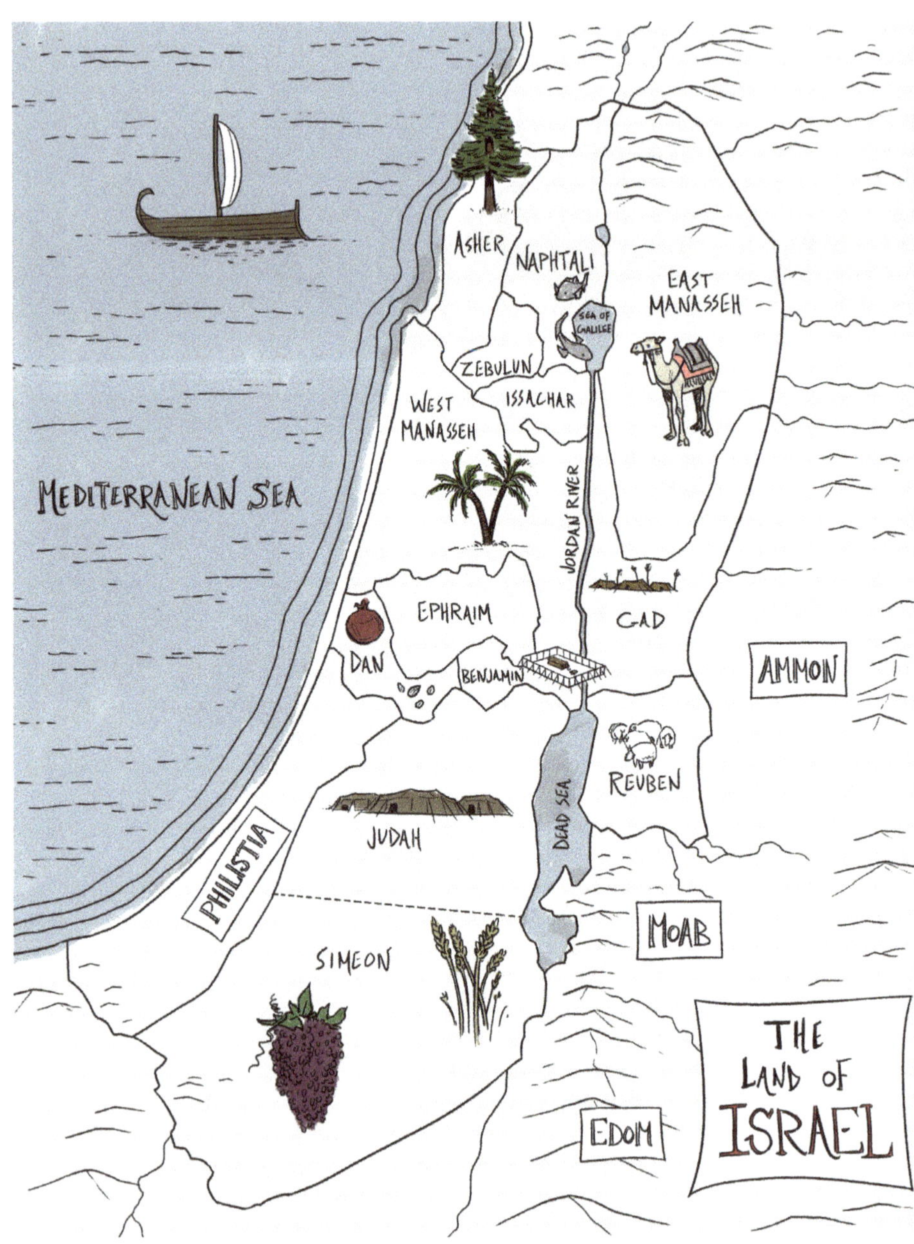

The Shema

The most central and important prayer in Judaism is the *Shema*. *Shema* (pronounced *sh'mah*) means "listen and do." It is the central prayer in Judaism because is reminds us of our covenant to hold tightly to the Torah and pass it on to our children.

שְׁמַע יִשְׂרָאֵל יְיָ אֱלֹהֵינוּ יְיָ אֶחָד

בָּרוּךְ שֵׁם כְּבוֹד מַלְכוּתוֹ לְעוֹלָם וָעֶד

***Shema Yisrael* ADONAI *Eloheinu*, ADONAI *echad*.**
Baruch shem k'vod malchuto l'olam va'ed.

Hear, Israel - The LORD our God, the LORD is one.
Blessed be His name, whose glorious kingdom is forever and ever. Amen.

Traditionally, the second line of this blessing is recited quieter than the first line.
It is also tradition to cover one's eyes with your right hand while reciting the Shema.

You shall love the LORD your God with all your heart, with all your soul, and with all your might. And these words which I am commanding you today shall be on your heart. You shall teach them dilligently to your children. You shall talk of them when you sit in your house and when you walk on the way, when you lie down and when you rise up. You shall bind them as a sign on your hand, and they shall be as frontlets between your eyes. You shall write them on the doorposts of your house and on your gates.

Deuteronomy 6:4-9

The Avinu

The *Avinu*, or Our Father, is the most well-known and loved ancient prayer in Yeshua-faith because it is the prayer our Rabbi Yeshua taught his disciples. Yeshua taught us to refer to God as our Father and this prayer shows us how to come before Him.

אָבִינוּ שֶׁבַּשָּׁמַיִם יִתְקַדַּשׁ שְׁמֶךָ: תָּבֹא מַלְכוּתֶךָ יֵעָשֶׂה רְצוֹנְךָ כַּאֲשֶׁר בַּשָּׁמַיִם גַּם בָּאָרֶץ: אֶת־לֶחֶם חֻקֵּנוּ תֶּן לָנוּ הַיּוֹם: וּמְחַל־לָנוּ עַל־חוֹבוֹתֵינוּ כַּאֲשֶׁר מָחַלְנוּ גַּם אֲנַחְנוּ לְחַיָּבֵינוּ: וְאַל־תְּבִיאֵנוּ לִידֵי נִסָּיוֹן כִּי אִם־תְּחַלְּצֵנוּ מִן־הָרָע. כִּי לְךָ הַמַּמְלָכָה וְהַגְּבוּרָה וְהַתִּפְאֶרֶת לְעוֹלְמֵי עוֹלָמִים אָמֵן

Avinu shebashamayim yitkadesh shmecha.
Tavo malchutecha, y'aseh retzonecha ka'asher bashamayim
gam b'aretz. Et lechem chukenu ten lanu hayom. U'mechal lanu
al chovoteinu, ka-asher machalnu gam anachnu lechayaveinu.
V'al t'viyeinu lidei nisayon ki im tachaltzeinu min hara. Ki lecha
hamamlecha v'hagevurah v'hatif'eret l'olmei olamim. Amen.

Our Father who is in heaven, may your name be sanctified. May your kingdom come; as your will is done in heaven, may it also be on earth. Give us the bread that is our allotment today. Pardon us our debts as we also have pardoned those indebted to us. Do not bring us into the hands of testing, but rescue us from what is evil. For yours is the kingdom and the power and the majesty, forever and ever. Amen.

Matthew 6:9-13

The Brachot L'Torah

The *Brachot L'Torah*, or The Blessings over the Torah, are the some of the most commonly-recited prayers in most synagogues - Messianic and Rabbinic. We hold the Torah in high esteem and are so thankful for God's Holy Word.

The Blessing before Reading the Torah:

בָּרְכוּ אֶת יְיָ הַמְבֹרָךְ | בָּרוּךְ יְיָ הַמְבֹרָךְ לְעוֹלָם וָעֶד

בָּרוּךְ אַתָּה יְיָ, אֱלֹהֵינוּ מֶלֶךְ הָעוֹלָם, אֲשֶׁר בָּחַר בָּנוּ מִכָּל הָעַמִּים וְנָתַן לָנוּ אֶת תּוֹרָתוֹ. בָּרוּךְ אַתָּה יְיָ, נוֹתֵן הַתּוֹרָה

(Leader) Barchu et ADONAI ham vorach.
(Everyone) Baruch ADONAI ham vorach le'olam va'ed.
(Leader) Baruch ADONAI ham vorach le'olam va'ed. Baruch atah ADONAI,
Eloheinu Melech ha'olam, asher bachar banu mikol ha'amim, v'natan lanu et Torato. Baruch atah ADONAI, notein haTorah. (Everyone) Amen.

Bless the LORD, the Blessed One.
Blessed is the LORD, the Blessed One for all eternity. Blessed are You, O LORD our God, King of the universe, who chose us from among all the peoples and gave us Your Torah. Blessed are You, O LORD, giver of the Torah. Amen.

The Blessing after Reading the Torah:

בָּרוּךְ אַתָּה יְיָ, אֱלֹהֵינוּ מֶלֶךְ הָעוֹלָם אֲשֶׁר נָתַן לָנוּ תּוֹרַת אֱמֶת וְחַיֵּי עוֹלָם נָטַע בְּתוֹכֵנוּ. בָּרוּךְ אַתָּה יְיָ, נוֹתֵן הַתּוֹרָה

(Leader) Baruch atah ADONAI, Eloheinu Melech ha'olam,
asher natan lanu Toraht emet, ve'ha'yay olam natah b'tocheynu.
Baruch atah ADONAI, notein haTorah. Amen.

Blessed are You, O LORD our God, King of the universe, who gave us the Torah of truth and planted everlasting life within us. Blessed are You, O LORD, giver of the Torah. Amen.

Erev Shabbat Blessings

The Erev Shabbat blessings are commonly recited in Jewish homes every Friday night and are also used to welcome in the *Mo'edim*, as they are special Shabbats. Notice that in each of these prayers we bless HaShem for the item, not the item itself.

The Erev Shabbat ceremony typically begins with the lighting of two candles shortly before sunset.

The Blessing for Lighting Shabbat Candles: *(traditionally said by women of the home)*

בָּרוּךְ אַתָּה יְיָ, אֱלֹהֵינוּ מֶלֶךְ הָעוֹלָם, אֲשֶׁר קִדְּשָׁנוּ בְּמִצְוֹתָיו,
וְצִוָּנוּ לְהַדְלִיק נֵר שֶׁל שַׁבָּת

Baruch atah Adonai, Eloheinu Melech ha'olam, asher kid'shanu b'mitzvotav v'tzivanu l'hadlik ner shel Shabbat.

Blessed are You, O Lord our God, King of the universe, who has sanctified us with His commandments and commanded us to kindle the Sabbath lights.

Alternative Shabbat Candle Blessing: *(preferred by some to keep the focus on Yeshua)*

בָּרוּךְ אַתָּה יְיָ, אֱלֹהֵינוּ מֶלֶךְ הָעוֹלָם, אֲשֶׁר קִדְּשָׁנוּ בְּמִצְוֹתָיו, וְצִוָּנוּ
לִהְיוֹת אוֹר לַגּוֹיִם וְנָתַן לָנוּ אֶת יֵשׁוּעַ מְשִׁיחֵנוּ אוֹר הָעוֹלָם

Baruch atah Adonai, Eloheinu Melech ha'olam, asher kid'shanu b'mitzvotav v'tzivanu liheyot or lagoyim v'natan lanu et Yeshua m'shicheinu or ha'olam.

Blessed are You, O Lord our God, King of the universe, who has sanctified us with His commandments and commanded us to be a light to the nations and gave us Yeshua our Messiah the light of the world.

After the candles are lit, the ceremony typically continues with the blessing of children by their father. Sometimes a song is sung here and the woman of the home is also often blessed by her husband. We aren't going to learn these blessings here, as they are said by the father (or if necessary, the mother) of the home.

HaGafen - Blessing over the Wine/Grape Juice:

בָּרוּךְ אַתָּה יְיָ אֱלֹהֵינוּ מֶלֶךְ הָעוֹלָם, בּוֹרֵא פְּרִי הַגֶּפֶן

Baruch atah Aᴅᴏɴᴀɪ, Eloheinu Melech ha'olam, borei p'ri hagefen.
(Amen)

Blessed are You, O Lᴏʀᴅ our God, King of the universe, creator of the fruit of the vine. (Amen)

Many add this blessing here, setting apart Shabbat as it begins.

Blessed are You, O Lᴏʀᴅ our God, King of the universe, who has sanctified us with His commandments, and chosen us, and given us in love and favor His holy Shabbat as an inheritance, as a remembrance of the act of creation. For this day is the beginning of all holy days, a remembrance of the Exodus from Egypt. You have chosen us and have blessed us from among all the nations, and with love and favor You have given us Your holy Shabbat. Blessed are You, O Lᴏʀᴅ, who sanctifies Shabbat. (Amen)

HaMotzi - Blessing over the Bread:

בָּרוּךְ אַתָּה יְיָ אֱלֹהֵינוּ מֶלֶךְ הָעוֹלָם, הַמּוֹצִיא לֶחֶם מִן הָאָרֶץ

Baruch atah Aᴅᴏɴᴀɪ, Eloheinu Melech ha'olam, hamotzi lechem min ha'aretz. (Amen)

Blessed are You, O Lᴏʀᴅ our God, King of the universe, who brings forth bread from the earth.

This blessing is traditionally recited over two challah loaves. The pieces of bread are then dipped in a little bit of salt, in memory of the Temple sacrifices that were offered with salt. This practice is the source of the expression "breaking bread" as a term for having a meal together.

These blessings may have also been part of the formation of the communion tradition and it is appropriate to remember Yeshua during this time.

After this blessing, a song or psalm can be recited and dinner begins!

Shabbat Shalom!

Havdalah Blessings

The Havdalah blessings are commonly recited in Jewish homes every Saturday night to formally end Shabbat and welcome the week ahead.

The Havdalah ceremony traditionally happens after 3 stars are visible in the night sky.

To set up for Havdalah, you will need a braided candle, a kiddush cup/goblet with a plate underneath, wine/juice, and a container of sweet spices like cinnamon, nutmeg, and cloves. Place the cup on the plate and fill it until it overflows. Light the candle and hold it or place in a holder.

Opening: (Isaiah 12:2-3)

Behold, God is my salvation! I will trust and will not be afraid. For the Lord Adonai is my strength and my song. He also has become my salvation. With joy you will draw water from the wells of salvation. Salvation belongs to the Lord; Your blessing is upon Your people. *Selah.*

HaGafen - Blessing over the Wine/Grape Juice:

בָּרוּךְ אַתָּה יְיָ אֱלֹהֵינוּ מֶלֶךְ הָעוֹלָם בּוֹרֵא פְּרִי הַגָּפֶן

Baruch atah Adonai, Eloheinu Melech ha'olam, borei p'ri hagefen. (Amen)

Blessed are You, O Lord our God, King of the universe, creator of the fruit of the vine. (Amen)

Minei V'samim - Blessing over the Spices:

בָּרוּךְ אַתָּה יְיָ, אֱלֹהֵינוּ מֶלֶךְ הָעוֹלָם, בּוֹרֵא מִינֵי בְשָׂמִים

Baruch atah Adonai, Eloheinu Melech ha'olam, borei minei v'samim. (Amen)

Blessed are You, O Lord our God, King of the universe, creator of various kinds of spices. (Amen)

At this time it is tradition to pass the spices around, giving each person a chance to smell their sweetness. This is one last reminder of the sweetness of Shabbat and a time to ask the Lord to carry its sweetness into the rest of the week, bringing the Sabbath rest we have in Messiah with us as we live out our days.

בָּרוּךְ אַתָּה יְיָ אֱלֹהֵינוּ מֶלֶךְ הָעוֹלָם, בּוֹרֵא מְאוֹרֵי הָאֵשׁ

**Baruch atah Adonai, Eloheinu Melech ha'olam, borei m'orei ha'eish.
(Amen)**

**Blessed are You, O Lord our God, King of the universe, creator of
the lights of fire.**

*At this time it is tradition to hold ones hand out toward the light of the candle, noticing
the distinction seen on the hand between the light and the shadows, giving a visual
representation of this next blessing.*

Closing - Separation:

בָּרוּךְ אַתָּה יְיָ אֱלֹהֵינוּ מֶלֶךְ הָעוֹלָם, הַמַּבְדִּיל בֵּין קֹדֶשׁ לְחוֹל,
בֵּין אוֹר לְחֹשֶׁךְ, בֵּין יִשְׂרָאֵל לָעַמִּים, בֵּין יוֹם הַשְּׁבִיעִי לְשֵׁשֶׁת
יְמֵי הַמַּעֲשֶׂה

בָּרוּךְ אַתָּה יְיָ, הַמַּבְדִּיל בֵּין קֹדֶשׁ לְחוֹל

**Baruch atah Adonai, Eloheinu Melech ha'olam, hamavdil bein kodesh
lechol, bein or lechoshech, bein Yisrael la'amim, bein yom hashevi'i
lesheshet yemei hama'aseh.**

Baruch atah Adonai, hamavdil bein kodesh lechol.

**Blessed are You, O Lord, our God, King of the universe, who
makes a distinction between what is holy and what is common,
between light and darkness, between Israel and the nations,
between the seventh day and the six days of creation. Blessed
are You, O Lord, who makes a distinction between what is holy
and what is common.**

*At this time you may pass and drink the wine/juice. This closes Havdalah and Shabbat. You
may wish to pray a prayer of blessing over your week to come. When finished, extinguish the
flame in the overflow of drink.*

Shavua Tov - Have a good week!

Chanukah Blessings

These are the prayers said when the menorah is lit each night of Chanukah.
On the first night, the *Shehechiyanu* is also said.

בָּרוּךְ אַתָּה יְיָ אֱלֹהֵינוּ מֶלֶךְ הָעוֹלָם אֲשֶׁר קִדְּשָׁנוּ בְּמִצְוֹתָיו וְצִוָּנוּ לְהַדְלִיק נֵר חֲנֻכָּה

בָּרוּךְ אַתָּה יְיָ אֱלֹהֵינוּ מֶלֶךְ הָעוֹלָם שֶׁעָשָׂה נִסִּים לַאֲבוֹתֵינוּ בַּיָּמִים הָהֵם בִּזְּמַן הַזֶּה

Baruch atah ADONAI, Eloheinu Melech ha'olam, asher kid'shanu b'mitzvotav v'tzivanu l'hadlik ner shel Chanukah.

Baruch atah ADONAI, Eloheinu Melech ha'olam, she'asah nisim la'avoteinu bayamim hahem bizman hazeh.

Blessed are You, O LORD our God, King of the universe, who has sanctified us with His commandments and commanded us to kindle the Chanukah lights.

Blessed are You, O LORD our God, King of the universe, who performed miracles for our forefathers in those days and at this season.

(Non-Jewish families may wish to alter these blessings by saying "inspired us" instead of "commanded us" and "His people Israel" instead of "our forefathers".)

On the first night, also add the Shehechiyanu!

Congratulations!

____

You have worked hard and learned all about the Torah this year!

We're proud of you for the lessons you studied, the verses you memorized, the Hebrew and liturgy you practiced, and the character you grew in this year. Mazel Tov!

______________________   ______________________
Teacher's Signature   Date